Praise for Criss Angel

"No magic show has ever been this dark. Criss Angel would eat David Copperfield's liver with a nice Chianti; he would spit a bat's head into David Blaine's face and kick the ass of Doug Henning's ghost. Every element of this show is disarmingly eerie."　　　　　—*Time Out New York*

"Fast paced and fun. . . . A splashy spectacle, engaging and eye-popping!"
　　　　　　　　　　　　　　　　　　　　　　　—*Daily News*

"A magician for the MTV generation."　　　　　　　　　　—NY1

"Extraordinary. . . . A spectacular mix of visionary magic and apocalyptic chic. This is the future and it can't come quickly enough." —Clive Barker

"Criss is a visionary. This man never ceases to amaze me with his creativeness."　　　　　　　—Jonathan Davis, lead singer of Korn

"Criss Angel has helped change the face of the A&E Network and has brought with him a whole new generation of viewers. His unique brand of magic, style, and intelligence makes him a modern day Houdini."
　　　　　—Abbe Raven, president and CEO, A&E Television Networks

"In my twenty-seven years in the music/entertainment business I have never met anyone more determined to make his mark than Criss Angel. He richly deserves all this success and more"
　　　　　　—Jason Flom, chairman and CEO, Virgin Records U.S.

"I don't think there is anyone in magic that has captured the public interest more right now than Criss Angel."　　　—Penn Jillette, Penn & Teller

"Criss Angel will be the biggest megastar in Las Vegas, and one of the biggest stars in the world. He combines the matinee idol good looks of a movie star, the coolness of a rock star, and the mystery of a 'Houdini for the New Millennium.'"
　　　　　—Felix Rappaport, president & COO, Luxor Resort and Casino

"Criss is going to be written up in the history books as one of the greatest magicians of the twenty-first century."　　　　　—Lance Burton

"An amazing illusionist! The best I've ever seen!"　　　—Howard Stern

"Criss Angel kicks magic in its tired old ass! A dynamic cross between Brandon Lee and Houdini that would make David Copperfield cry for his memory."　　　　　　　　　　　　　　　　　—Rob Zombie

"Greatness is he who reminds you of no

CRISS ANGEL
MINDFREAK ™

Criss Angel
WITH LAURA MORTON

40 MINDFREAKS
by Criss Angel and Richard Kaufman

HARPER

ENTERTAINMENT
An Imprint of HarperCollinsPublishers

HARPER ⬤ ENTERTAINMENT

A HARDCOVER EDITION OF THIS BOOK WAS PUBLISHED IN 2007 BY HARPERENTERTAINMENT, AN
IMPRINT OF HARPERCOLLINS PUBLISHERS.

FIRST HARPER PAPERBACK PUBLISHED 2008.

COVER ART AND INTERIOR ART DESIGNED BY CRISS ANGEL
AND STEPHANIE LYNN EVANS OF APWI

THE LIBRARY OF CONGRESS HAS CATALOGUED THE HARDCOVER EDITION AS FOLLOWS:

ANGEL, CRISS.
MINDFREAK : SECRET REVELATIONS / CRISS ANGEL.—1ST ED.
P. CM.
ISBN 978-0-06-113761-7
ISBN-10: 0-06-113761-8
1. ANGEL, CRISS. 2. MAGICIANS—UNITED STATES—BIBLIOGRAPHY.
3. MINDFREAK (TELEVISION PROGRAM) I. TITLE

GV1545.A54A3 2007
793.8092—DC22
[B]   2006052513

ISBN 978-0-06-113762-4 (PBK.)

08 09 10 11 12 ID/RRD 10 9 8 7 6 5 4 3 2 1

To my mother,

Dimitra,

and in eternal loving memory of my father,

John Sarantakos

Love Lives Forever . . .

Without the love, support, and guidance of my family,
I would have never been able to live my dreams.

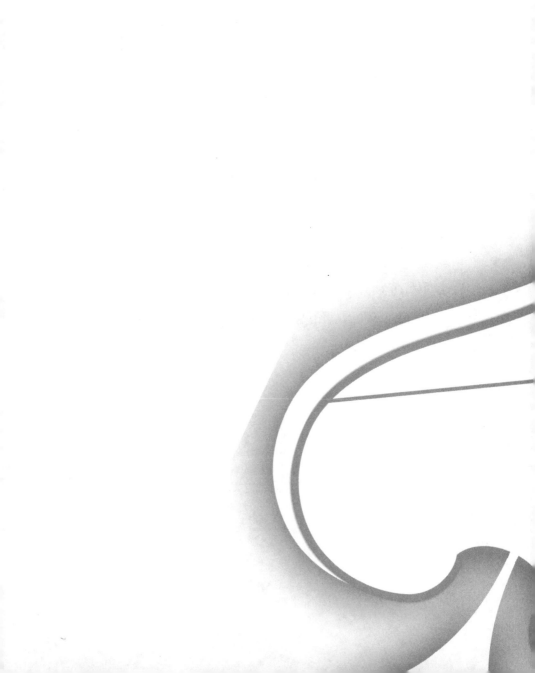

CONTENTS

Part I

Part I

Indescribable pain shoots through my flesh as, attached to four fishhooks, a helicopter raises me more than 1,000 feet in the air.

INTRODUCTION

I was three hours into the desert outside Las Vegas. I arrived at our location in the pitch black of night, so I had no sense of the beauty that surrounded me. It's the last week of shooting the first season of my television show, *MINDFREAK*, and I am exhausted. I need a break from the nonstop grind of working twenty-two-hour days for the past several months—the physical demands I had placed on my body were finally taking a toll. I only have this one last demonstration left to shoot, but it is by far the most challenging I've attempted all season. Tomorrow I will face an extreme version of a body suspension, something I have successfully done two times before. I plan to retire it from my act after tomorrow's final demonstration, which is going to take place over the spectacular mountains and canyons of the Valley of Fire.

I chose to come to the Nevada desert by motorcycle and camp out with my family, friends, and crew. I rode my Harley, joined by my brother Costa and my cousin George who rode their bikes, too. I wanted to clear my mind and get away from the chaos and craziness that has become my life. If I'm going to be successful, it's important my head be in the right place. After all, what I'm about to do, no man has ever attempted before. In the morning, someone will place four 8 gauge hooks across the top of my back, from shoulder to shoulder. Then I'll suspend my body in the upright position from a helicopter, which will fly with me dangling below, hanging by my flesh for a full twenty minutes over the Valley of Fire. Some might question why I would want to do this. Am I crazy? Am I a masochist? Do I have some kind of death wish? No. I want to do this to prove to myself that first place isn't enough. Being number one doesn't necessarily mean being the best. I have an innate need to push myself to places others only dream of, places some might consider a living nightmare.

The body suspension is a complete demonstration of how my mind can control pain in my body. Through years of training my mind, body, and spirit to work in harmony, I have developed methods to overcome all forms of fear, pain, and anxiety. In some cultures, this type of body piercing and demonstration is a rite of passage from childhood to adulthood. Tomorrow, it will be a ritualistic passage for me as well. If I'm successful, I will have proved I can take the smallest seed of an idea, impossible as it seems, and turn it into a real live event.

I already showed the world I could do the body suspension when I performed it live in 2002, hanging for six hours in Times Square. That time I used eight hooks and was suspended in the "Superman" position. I practiced this demonstration once before that performance, so I knew I could accomplish it for the Times Square suspension. For the desert suspension, I decided to do something different—something even the experts who trained me said couldn't be done. It had to be radical and extreme—especially because this would definitely be my last suspension. It had to be big.

When I awoke, I found myself surrounded by the intense beauty of the desert. It looked like the surface of Mars. I was in awe. It was a gorgeous morning in an incredible setting of red rock formations and desert sand. It was perfect. I am a man whose ego is never satisfied, but I also have a lot at risk when I attempt to do something this dangerous. Failure is not an option. That morning I was still unsure about using four, six, or eight hooks. I always push the envelope and today was no

BEFORE ANY DEMONSTRATION I NEED A MOMENT ALONE TO GATHER
MY THOUGHTS.

exception. The hooks have nuts and bolts to secure once they've been
inserted through the skin. Once locked, there was no way they would
slip through my flesh. After evaluating my options and various factors,
there was no doubt in my mind what the perfect setup would be: four
hooks in the upright or "suicide" position; two helicopters; the Valley
of Fire ... I was ready. Let's do it.

I chose not to take painkillers or use a numbing cream for the piercing: I wanted to experience the entire process without escaping the sensations. I lay facedown on a table so the hooks could be inserted; there
was pain, but it was tolerable. I was feeling positive, really strong—like
it was going to be a breeze. My confidence was high. As I've mentioned,
I had been through this before, so I knew what to expect. Next, I left
for the site, where I would be strung up to a truss to hang for fifteen to
twenty minutes. I needed to get used to the sensation of the four hooks

GETTING INTO THE MIND-SET WHILE LISTENING TO "RIGHT NOW"
BY KORN.

and feel the balance of my body weight distribution. I needed to get totally comfortable before the helicopter arrived and I was plucked off the desert floor.

As time passed, I hadn't found my comfort zone, but the crew wanted to hook me up to the helicopter. I felt rushed. I don't respond well when people try to pressure me, because only I know when my mind, body, and spirit are aligned. I'm not ready. I push myself harder than anyone. I know when I'm good to go. Right now, I was in a bad place. I was swinging back and forth, my feet inches off the ground, while my core body temperature had dropped and I had broken into a cold sweat. I'm told I was pale white, like I was going to pass out. I couldn't do it. I needed to come down. I wanted to feel my bare feet on the rocks and dirt. Historically, anyone who has tried something like this, if they go down, they don't go back up.

My confidence was waning. I felt like a prizefighter who goes into the big fight thinking he's going to beat the shit out of someone and ends up getting knocked out in the first round. I had to pull myself together if I wanted to win this battle, even if I didn't feel strong. Even if I was intimidated and overwhelmed, I had so much on the line. Money, ego, my own expectations for myself, and the idea that so many other people were counting on me.

Whenever I need to silence my inner thoughts, I grab my iPod. I immediately found two of my favorite Korn songs, "Right Now" and "Alone I Break," and began to psych myself up. I had to deal with this like any other obstacle. I'd find a way to get through it.

"Let's do it!" I yelled. Thunderous, heart-pounding music was blasting in my ears, rhythmically timed to the thumping of my heart. It was turning into a very hot desert day. The sun was beating down on my bare chest. For thirty minutes, I would be a miserable human being, but I told myself that my suffering was temporary. All I could think was, "I've got to do this." There was no turning back. In my mind, the worst-case scenario was a half hour of agony. I knew I could get through that.

Thoughts of my father swirled in my head like the blades of the hovering helicopters. His death had had a profound impact on my life. I began to think about his sixtieth birthday party—the last we would celebrate together before he died. It was a happy memory, one that wasn't tied to his pain and suffering toward the end. Dad didn't have a choice about his suffering and death. His cancer chose him. As for me, I was choosing to put myself in the scenario. My father had always been my greatest motivation and positive guiding force, and today was no exception. His energy and spirit were with me. I began to feed off that intensity building in my family, friends, and crew members who came to support me in this attempt to conquer the Valley of Fire. I didn't want to disappoint anyone—most important, myself. This demonstration would have to kill me before I would allow myself to fail. I would never be able to live with myself if I gave up. I had to do it.

I took my time. When I was ready, I turned to the camera that had captured every moment for TV and said, *"I'm Criss Fuckin' Angel."*

It wasn't planned, but it was exactly how I felt in that moment. I was like Superman. The adrenaline was kicking in. I wanted to do this quickly and well and never go through it again.

The helicopter landed at base camp. The pilots were the best in the business. They had done countless films and knew exactly how to work in tandem to keep me safe while recording every second. We were ready to do this.

The wind suddenly kicked up, and in practice runs, we had failed to calculate the extra force of the second helicopter—dirt and debris were flying everywhere. But I put that all out of my mind. The choppers hovered above, holding remarkably steady while the crew was trying to hook me up to the rig that would connect me to the helicopter. Finally, the ground crew locked me in. There was no turning back.

I immediately started swinging back and forth, causing my body weight to be unevenly distributed among the four hooks. The pain from being lifted was the worst pain I have ever felt. I let out a bloodcurdling scream. It was primal. It took me back to when I was a kid. I thought about all of the times I passed out when my family doctor, Dr. Michael Lemonedes, tried to take blood from my arm. I could never have imagined this moment then. Never.

Pain is a state of mind. I needed to become numb to it. My flesh was separating from my body. It was the most intense sensation. I loved it and I hated it. I was so pumped up, the adrenaline now rushing through my body like a raging river. I continued to scream—to let out and let go of my pain.

The helicopter drifted upward. I was seeing the world from more than a thousand feet above the ground. I was experiencing a completely different perspective on the Valley of Fire, on the planet Earth, than any other human being has ever experienced before. I was flying—my arms extended, palms up, and my ankles crossed. I felt invincible.

I wanted to enjoy this—to absorb it, take it in, and appreciate this

YEAH, I WAS DOING IT! THE FIRST PERSON EVER TO DO SUCH A
DEMONSTRATION.

9

GETTING DOWN FROM THOSE ROPES WAS LIKE A
RELIGIOUS EXPERIENCE.

moment because I was never going to be here again. While music
pumped from my iPod, I felt so insignificant. I was like a grain of sand
in the desert—a speck in this vast, magnificent landscape. It was ethe-
real. The body suspension was as close to an out-of-body experience
as I have ever had. It wasn't me. It was something far bigger than me
hanging that day.

The turbulence and downdraft from the second chopper were causing me to swing side to side instead of front to back, which meant my
body weight was being shifted from four hooks to one, then two, and so
on. My serenity was quickly broken by the pain; my screams could easily be heard over the sound of the helicopter. As I came over the ridge
my brothers had climbed to the top of the mountain to cheer me on;
they could hear me let out a deep, loud, fantastic shout.

"CRISS FLEW OVER US in what was called the
'tableau' pose, where his arms are straight out to

his sides, palms up, and his ankles crossed. A lot of
people thought he was imitating Christ on a cross.
As long as he stayed in that pose, we knew HE WAS
ALL RIGHT. If he put his arms down that was our cue
that something was wrong and to get him down.
It was a beautiful experience."

Costa, my brother

It was incredible. It was life-altering. Not just for me, but for everyone there that day. When the helicopter set me down, there was a
euphoria we all shared. We were all emotional, crying, realizing all of
the angst, frustration, and extreme fatigue that had built up over the
course of the long season. The emotional impact affected everyone.

I know my family worries about me and my insane attempts at
life-or-death situations. I wouldn't let my mother attend this particular
demonstration because I knew she'd never have been able to cope with
the extreme atmosphere. I called her immediately after and told her
how much I loved her, that it was done, and that I was safe.

"I don't know how **my heart is so strong**.
My doctor told me he wanted to check my heart
to make sure I could **withstand the stress**
of watching my son go through all of his crazy
demonstrations. I'm happy to report I have *a heart
younger than a thirty-five-year-old.* When I
watch Christopher doing dangerous things, it's very
hard. IT'S REAL. I'm a mother who would crawl
through the mud to pull my son out from being

buried alive if I thought he was dying. There have been many times, I was close."

Dimitra, my mom

As an artist, I can be a little selfish at times. My first aim is to please myself, and in turn, if my art pleases others, then that makes it even more special. I do what I do so I can make my own choices. I never want anyone telling me what to do. I don't consider myself to be the slightest bit of a daredevil, because I don't do stupid things. Though there are real risks in everything I attempt, I am highly trained and very methodical about doing my due diligence so I avoid getting hurt. I can spend months training my mind and body to be ready for a demonstration like the body suspension. I have to be certain my entire team is ready, too—and it takes a large group of people to help me pull off the impossible.

I have never thought of what I do as magic or myself as a magician. What I do pushes the limits of magic and traditional magicians. I refer to all of my performances as *demonstrations* rather than "tricks" because they are a compilation of so many different techniques rolled into one overall experience. It's a neutral term that allows me to blur the line between reality and illusion.

A lot of what I do is real, and much of what I do is an illusion. It's up to you to decipher which is which. I willingly choose to put myself in situations that are traumatic, challenging, brutal tests of strength and spirit. That's why I am most proud of the helicopter suspension. It is one of the best examples of my unwavering perseverance, my unwavering inner and outer strength, and the extreme power of my mental makeup both as a performer and as a man. It was truly a test of my mind, body, and spirit. I made a life choice many years ago to rise above the traditional expectations of reality and possibility.

The debate of real versus illusion has always intrigued me. It's what keeps my job interesting and fulfilling. If I told you how I did all of my demonstrations, it would take away so much of the total experience for you. Great magic captivates an audience with a simple plot—a situation that provokes a thoughtful challenge, provides conflict, and offers a distinct climax and surprise. Look, obviously I can't make an elephant disappear, but I can create the illusion that the elephant vanished right before your eyes. Houdini's Vanishing Elephant trick was the result of more than a half century of experiments by stage magicians in France, England, and the United States. Houdini purchased the secret and it became synonymous with one of the greatest legends in magic.

"THE SPHINX IS a masterpiece in the
Sahara Desert and cannot be described as anything
other than an illusion. The Sphinx has not moved,
but the men who built it have all DISAPPEARED
WITHOUT
A TRACE, like a midday mirage."

Italo Calvino

The art that is most real to me is the art I invent in my head. Much like Calvino's Sphinx, sometimes my art is just an illusion—or is it? Why is it necessary that the images I create be credible? If my demonstrations entertain, provoke emotion, excite, aggravate, confuse, or baffle, isn't that what art is supposed to do? The art of illusion is finding external suggestions that help you process false memories. Corroboration of an event by another person only adds to the process of making you believe what I choose to make you see.

"MY HEART IS USUALLY IN MY THROAT when
I watch Criss perform. Sometimes, I feel like a
parent, because it's really my responsibility to keep
him alive. **He's fearless,** but the rest of us—crew,
friends, and family—**we're scared to death.**"

Michael Blum,
executive producer, MINDFREAK

When I am out there, whether on the street or in front of an audience doing a live show, I control the audience, their reactions, their experience, and their joy. I control the entire scenario, but I make the audience or spectators feel like they're completely in control. A great performer allows his audiences to believe they are making their own choices. Our society is based on control and power—some good, some bad. When you're able to manipulate one's senses you have total control of that situation. It's a chess game of sorts. By the end of the demonstration, I think most people have been MINDFREAKed. They're blown away by what they've just experienced. They're different than they were before they witnessed what they believed to be inconceivable, impossible, and out of the question. That's what makes performing like a drug to me.

When I first started performing, I intentionally aimed to do radical things. I believed that would be a key element in my success. Take a look at history, people like Elvis Presley, the Beatles, Kiss, Madonna; or, for you early-stage magician fans, there was David Devant, T. Nelson Downs, P. T. Selbit, John Nevil Maskelyne, and Jean-Eugène Robert-Houdin. They're all performers who pushed the limits of their art. I wanted to be like them, to go to the extreme and do something completely different than the world of magic has ever known. I am absolutely obsessed with creating art and generating unforgettable experiences that get people's attention.

"I have ***the best way*** of telling who the most popular magician is. Fifteen years ago, **I was only asked about David Copperfield**; five years ago, I was only asked about David Blaine; and now **I am only asked about Criss Angel**."

Penn Jillette

Art is something that encourages us to remember or to imagine. I make my living in a high-risk industry, and I must constantly prove I am the original MINDFREAK! I'm a dreamer. I don't always know if something is going to work a hundred percent of the time. That's what gets me off. That uncertainty and the challenge of pulling off a demonstration unlike anything attempted before. I imagine something, figure out how to make it real, and then pull it out of my metaphorical sleeve in front of millions of people. Call it whatever you want, but for me that's the ultimate in true performance art.

As my curiosity continued to grow, everything about magic and art began to interest me. I became fascinated by pop culture and the infiltration of surreal elements in my work. In fact, I often call my art "surreality" because it seamlessly blends the real and the surreal, bringing the audience into a world that doesn't really exist. But in that moment it is real.

As a storyteller, I must absolutely believe in what I'm making you believe so you can identify with it. My demonstrations become a microscopic complete world. My work is to make you believe that anything is possible. It's not just an expression; it's a way of being. It's how I live. I want to share all aspects of my story with you so you can get an inside view on Criss Angel, both MINDFREAK and Man. My journey has been long, thrilling, sometimes disappointing, but always worth-it-traveled road. It has taken me a lifetime to create this long narrative that threads the fabric of my work together with my search, on various levels, for a personal style, coherence, essence, and a greater spontaneity, to live the expression of my art. Ultimately it has been a search for the truest, most authentic part of myself, which I have captured over the years through my performances and now in the pages of this book. While you won't learn all the secrets behind my demonstrations, I think you'll walk away feeling like you've had the chance to get to know me a little better. Some of what you read may surprise you—I hope it entertains you. My goal has always been to leave you, my audience, and in this case, my reader, satisfied while raising questions that provoke more thought, more controversy, and a desire, at least on a personal level, to live to your greatest potential. So, with the words with which I begin every show, I will begin my book: Are you ready?

CHAPTER ONE

BEHIND
CLOSED DOORS

THE FIRST TIME PERFORMING THE BODY SUSPENSION
IN THE SUPERMAN POSITION IN TIMES SQUARE. I WAS
HANGING FOR ALMOST SIX HOURS.

Eleanor Roosevelt once said, "You gain strength, courage, and confidence by every experience in which you really stop to look fear in the face. You are able to say to yourself, 'I lived through this horror. I can take the next thing that comes along.' . . . *You must do the thing you think you cannot do.*" I have mentally overcome situations most of you would be terrified to ever attempt: heights, fire, needles, spiders, snakes, angry monkeys, being shot, being hit by a car, going blind—you name it, I have been in a situation where I have had to mentally overcome my inherent fears to do my job. Everybody always asks me, "How do you do it?"

I'm fearless. I always try to focus on the worst thing that could happen—and for me the answer is always the same.

Death.

I accept death. So what do I fear if I don't fear death?

Nothing.

My problem-solving skills allow me to create and demonstrate my art at a higher caliber and separate myself from being average, dull, mundane, and boring. It has always been my mantra that every one of my demonstrations must be able to be done live. I am a street performer as much as I am a stage performer. Yes, I have a television show, but every trick, every MINDFREAK you see, I can do live. Television is a wonderful way to deliver my art, but for all of the conspiracy theorists out there, it allows room for doubt. The strangest thing about my television show is that the things people think are real are not and the things people believe are fake are totally authentic. That makes for some very challenging and thought-provoking television and entertainment.

The body suspension episode is probably one of the shows people speculate on the most. Was it real? Was I wearing some type of prosthetic like a skin suit? Whenever I come up with an idea for a demonstration, I aim for something I know will have a dramatic impact and will be perceived as engaging. I want to get people excited by what they see—to make them think, squirm, and get nervous, but I always want them to stay connected to what I'm doing. The details of a demonstration are always secondary. The more emotional, mental, and physical a demonstration is for me to endure, the bigger the impact for you, the audience. As an artist, that's the perfect equation for the biggest bang—the greatest impression.

The first time I thought about attempting a body suspension was after watching a documentary on rites-of-passage ceremonies from other cultures. I was completely intrigued by what these people put their bodies through. One of the experts on the show was a body-piercing professional from Texas named Allen Faulkner, who is legendary in the world of piercing and suspension techniques. He hosts the equivalent of "suspension raves" for people who are interested in trying body suspension. Hundreds of people show up to a remote warehouse location, and, under his strict supervision and expertise, they attempt to become human mobiles. After watching the documentary, I immediately researched Allen on the Internet and came across his website. If I was going to do this, I needed to find someone who was an authority on this technique; Allen was the perfect guy for the job. I explained my concept to him, and he told me he'd be interested in helping me out.

I went to Texas to meet Allen and experienced a body suspension for the first time. I brought a camera crew with me to record every moment. Although I was training to do this demonstration several months later in Times Square for a television special, I wanted to practice and go through a suspension once so I'd know what to expect.

The night before my first "practice" suspension, Allen warned me not to drink any alcohol—he reminded me that alcohol thins out your blood and that can cause excessive bleeding. I was really concerned about what I should eat, too. He suggested something hardy but not greasy. I opted for some grilled chicken. My crew and I went to a TGI Friday's, where I sat, feeling a little anxious about the unexpected nature of doing a body suspension.

What would it feel like?

What was going to happen?

What would the pain of the giant fishhooks going into my skin feel like?

"Before our father's illness, Christopher wouldn't let the doctor **take blood** from his arm. He would get queasy and pass out! HE DIDN'T LIKE BLOOD OR NEEDLES AT ALL."

J. D., my brother

Up to this point, I had had minimal experiences with piercing (just my ears). Let me go on record and say that a pierced ear is not even in the same galaxy as a body piercing, especially eight 8 gauge salmon fishhooks that were about to be embedded into my skin. Six were going to be inserted into my back, and two into my calves. I would not take painkillers or any other sedative. I had to feel the pain. It was part of the experience. I've never formally trained for pain management, but I have a good understanding of how to conquer it. I just analyze the pain, feel it in the moment, and then mentally become numb to it.

I got to the warehouse and began to wonder what I'd gotten myself into. I was told to lie facedown on a gurney that had been carefully sterilized. Allen and the rest of the pierce team placed surgical masks over their faces, looking very much like doctors about to perform a major surgical procedure, except they were slightly more tattooed and pierced than any doctor I had ever met. They marked the points of insertion on my back and legs with a blue Sharpie pen. They cleansed my skin, put a sanitizing gel on each spot, and began.

"Are you ready, Criss?"

"I think so."

"Breathe. It's very important to breathe."

I was familiar with various breathing techniques from other demonstrations and experiences, so I knew focusing on my breathing would be very helpful in diverting my attention from the intense pain. I had to redirect my attention to something that was pleasurable.

My brother Costa and my production designer, John Farrell, were with me. I was grateful for their presence, especially in this moment. I know it's hard for my family to witness most of the strains I put on my body. Today would be no exception.

I took a deep breath in and began to slowly release it as they pulled my skin from my back, pinching it evenly on both sides and inserted the first of eight needles, which then pulled the hooks through the skin. They look for areas of the skin with more elasticity, to prevent excessive scarring. They put two hooks in at a time so the procedure goes twice as fast and so that the pain is kept even and equal at the two entry points. The piercing is similar to poking a sharp object through Styrofoam. You can feel the hook go in, there's a slight push, and suddenly it goes all the way through. It is a bizarre feeling. At first, there's a huge amount of pain, but once the needle goes through the skin, the pain stops. I held on to the gurney, focused on my breathing, and tried to ignore how startling this was to my body.

If you put the hooks in too shallow, they will rip right through the skin. If you put them in too deep, it can cause permanent muscle damage. My calves were by far the most painful of the eight hooks. You have less elasticity in your calves than you do in your back, especially if you are in good physical condition. If you have less body fat, there's less skin to work with for the piercing. One of the needles slipped out of Allen's hand, which meant he had to regroup and start again on that particular leg. The entire piercing took less than five minutes, though it was pretty rough.

It was time to stand up. Having eight hooks in your skin is a strange sensation. Looking at the prestrung rigging above my head was downright scary. I was planning to hang in the Superman position, as if I were flying. They attached the rope, which is actually parachute cord, hook by hook, until all eight were connected in one continuous line to the rig. They use one line to make sure body weight is distributed evenly over the cord. If they were to use individual lines, each one could potentially be at a slightly different tension so that any one hook—or all eight—would be carrying a different weight. I had no idea the hardest part was still to come.

I lay back down on the gurney, my head facedown in the cradle. Allen came to the front to hold my hands as the rest of his guys began pulling me up off the table. I felt like an engine being lifted out of a car. This was, by far, the most excruciatingly painful part of the process, because your skin is essentially separating from your body's muscles and tissue. I immediately went into shock. I was concerned I would vomit, which would have been horribly painful, as I was now suspended a few feet in the air. My body temperature couldn't regulate itself. I went from being intensely hot to shivering cold and then hot again. I asked for a fan to cool me down as sweat poured off my body.

The human contact with Allen was crucial. It kept me aware and conscious. He was no longer holding my hands, but was now lightly supporting them with his so I knew he was still there. If and when he let go, I would know that I was hanging one hundred percent on my own. The thought of that was a little freaky to me at first, but it began to pass.

I never allow myself, my mind, or my thoughts to take me to those places. I can't allow myself to get psyched-out, to give in to the worry, the pain, or the fear. I would not let my mind and spirit give in to the physical pain and pull being placed on my body.

Instead, I began to focus on the pain. I embraced and accepted it. I analyzed the sensation of it.

What is pain?

It's a state of mind. It's how you're feeling. It's a sensation—the same as pleasure. I am not equating pain to pleasure. I am only drawing a comparison in that they are both feelings. If pleasure is good, why is pain bad?

I began to play games with my thoughts. I often mess with my sense of reality and what particular words really mean. Each of us is conditioned to react to certain sensations from the time we are babies. When a child falls, if the parent's response is one of panic and angst, the child begins to cry, even if the child is not hurt. Likewise, when that child falls, and the parent's reaction is nonresponsive, the child gets up and keeps playing. We have been programmed to assume that if you fall, you will feel pain. That isn't necessarily true. I tell myself I am greater than the pain. I can endure it and become one with it.

You can overcome anything when your mind is more powerful than your emotions. I have never had to forgo a demonstration because I was too uncomfortable, in too much pain, or feeling too claustrophobic to complete the task. Unprepared? For sure. But never mentally unable. That would be disaster.

You control everything you think, feel, say, how you act, and how you respond. If you really understand who you are, and I mean who you truly are, then you already understand how to be successful in the things you want to accomplish, whether it's losing weight or quitting smoking. That knowledge guides me throughout every demonstration I attempt. I'm not suggesting this technique works for everyone, but it works for me.

Allen finally let go of my hands, and suddenly I was okay. I was alive and fully aware of my sensations. I was uncomfortable, but it wasn't unmanageable. The nausea had passed. My body temperature was settled. The worst was behind me. My mind-set began to shift.

"I'm doing it. I'm really doing it."

I hung for three hours. I felt the greatest sense of accomplishment for doing something that a lot of other people would say is just a stupid act that has no merit or meaning, which in their lives may be completely true. But this was not about the act. It was about me—my body, my brain, my spirit, and the connection of all three, which could not be broken. When they brought me down off the rig, after removing the hooks, I proudly wore the holes in my back and legs as my personal badges of honor. They were my war wounds.

Whether completing a body suspension for three hours or being buried alive beneath thousands of pounds of dirt, every demonstration I do requires a complete, symbiotic coming together of mind over matter, which gives me the greatest feeling of complete victory in the face of defeat.

After you come down off the suspension rig and the hooks are removed, one final assault on the body takes place. You have to properly burp the skin. When the skin is pulled from the body, air gets trapped beneath the surface. If you don't get rid of that excess air, it takes a lot longer to recover and it is extremely painful. Burping the skin is essential on several levels. First, the pain from the trapped air is excruciating. The release of the air is comforting and feels good—you *want* to get it out. Second, you have to remove the air to prevent possible blood clots. Allen and his team slowly massaged my back and legs, gently pushing the excess air to the surface of each hole. The sound is similar to the sound a water bed makes when you empty it of air. When burping the skin, the excess air sometimes gets mixed with blood, creating a mini volcanolike response through the skin. It's really gross. In fact, there were a few people on the set who almost passed out from the shocking image of this explosion from my back. It was too disgusting to air on television. Costa continued to massage and burp my skin on our flight back to New York, and for several days after, to hurry along my recovery.

After the suspension, I went for a walk, alone, in search of something to eat. I wanted to try and take in what I had just done. I felt so strong and powerful. I'm a sucker for junk food. I love chocolate chip cookies, candy, soda—all the stuff I know I shouldn't eat. I found a convenience store alongside the road. I went in and celebrated what I had just accomplished by allowing myself to indulge in all the junk food I could handle. It was a small bonus compared to the reward of doing it.

After my victory in Texas, I was ready to attempt the body suspension for my first television special. Once again, I was going to hang in the Superman position, suspended five feet off the ground by eight large fishhooks for six hours—the longest anyone has ever been suspended. Again, the hooks were placed evenly on both sides of my body; two in my shoulders, two in my midback region, two in my lower back, and two in my calves.

There was some resistance to doing this demonstration in a post–9/11 New York City. I wasn't sure people were ready to see a guy hanging by fishhooks on the corner of Forty-third and Broadway. But, like everything I do, it was time to push the limits of my performance and the boundaries of what people were ready to see. I had to generate some noise to blow any of my competitors out of the water. To do that, I needed to be radical and hard-core.

I hung in Times Square for almost six hours. Tens of thousands of people came to see me. Throughout my suspension, I witnessed a wide range of reactions. I knew people would doubt the validity of the suspension or think it was some type of illusion, but I had nothing to hide. It was purely authentic—what you see is what you get. Some people claimed I wore a skin suit or some kind of false skin. I'd like to know what a skin suit is, because I'd happily sign up for one. It would have been a hell of a lot easier! Some people even suggested I was a hologram, so I began to spin and do acrobatics to make people realize I wasn't some projected image or a guy in some meditative state just hanging there. Just in case you were one of those people doubting that demonstration, I ripped the skin on my calf with one of the hooks from doing too many moves. I began to bleed pretty profusely, until the paramedics thought I might be in real danger and insisted I be brought down and examined. They were worried that my body was in shock and unable to regulate my body temperature and blood pressure. And, in case you're wondering, I still bare the scars of those fishhooks today.

CHAPTER TWO

THE
EARLY DAYS

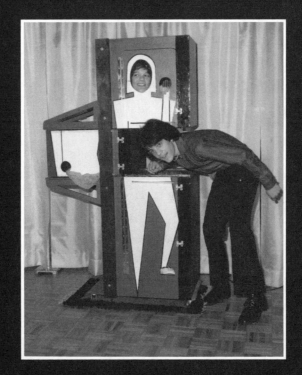

PERFORMING ZIG-ZAG AT AGE FOURTEEN.

I was born the youngest of three boys in Long Island, New York. I always had a need to follow in my older brothers' footsteps in everything they did. It didn't matter what they were up to, I had to do it, too. When J. D. and Costa were learning to play various musical instruments, I asked my mom and dad if I could take music lessons, too, even though I was just six years old. They played football and baseball. I was too young to play on their teams, but their coaches arranged for me to play for the other teams. Growing up, my mother used to tell my father that there was something special about me. She always knew I had a gift to make people happy. Whatever I got involved in, I tried to be the best. Being number one has always been important.

"There's always been *something extraordinary about Christopher.* He had a look, an expression on his face, the way he smiled—HE WAS CAPTIVATING, even as a baby. All three of my boys have beautiful qualities and are great guys, but Christopher always had that **something extra that made him special.**

I used to tell my husband, '*This kid* is going to be something someday.' I wasn't sure what, but I ALWAYS KNEW HE'D BE VERY SUCCESSFUL."

Dimitra, my mom

When I was seven, my mother's sister, Stella, came to our house with her son. She called my cousin and me over so she could do a card trick for us. Afterward she asked us to guess how it was done. My cousin walked away completely uninterested in the impossibility of what we saw because he already knew how to do the trick. I begged him to tell me, but he wouldn't. It just boggled my mind. I had to know how she did it. I bugged Aunt Stella for hours.

"C'mon Aunt Stella. You've got to show me."

She kept me hanging.

"C'mon. Please show me." I begged and begged until she couldn't

COSTA, MOM (HOLDING ME), AND J. D.

A DAY I WISH I COULD REMEMBER.

I STARTED PLAYING DRUMS AND, BELIEVE IT OR NOT, THE ACCORDION AT AGE SIX. SOON AFTER, I DROPPED THE ACCORDION. THANK GOD. . . .

take another minute of my asking and finally gave in. From that day on, I was hooked. Once she shared the secret of the trick, I felt this incredible sense of power that an adult didn't understand how it worked, but *I* did. It was very enticing. I became extremely fascinated by magic, so much so that a few years later, I told my mom and dad I didn't want clothes or toys for Christmas. I just wanted magic tricks. I loved magic and music. Both were all I could think about.

My parents looked at each other with that "Oh no, what have we done?" look. The thought of my becoming a professional magician was unbearable for them. They had hoped their three sons would go to college and become doctors or lawyers—but not a magician! I was consumed with magic and performing. I spent endless hours reading books at the library, studying magicians and their legacies. When my friends were all going out on weekends, I stayed home to create little models of the stage I wanted built for my show when I got older. I built it out of toothpicks, drawing elaborate plans and ideas on endless pieces of paper my mom found strewn all over my bedroom. My mind never stopped thinking about magic.

My intense drive, insatiable hunger, and quest for success have been part of my personality from the day I was born. I so desperately wanted to achieve my dreams, I didn't care how it came. I'd do whatever I could to be in front of an audience. I played the accordion (not very well) and drums (I was pretty good for my age) and sang (experimented with it). I could do magic (trying to find myself), and I loved performing (that came the most natural to me.) Throughout my childhood and into my early teen years, I regularly made the trek from our home in Long Island, New York, to Manhattan, to go on auditions and go-see's. I wanted to do it all—model, act, juggle, ride a unicycle, eat cereal in front of the camera—whatever it took to do this for a living. My approach to everything has always been to say "Yes, I can do that" and then figure out how to make it happen. I was willing to sacrifice my childhood, my friends, and my personal life so I could pursue my passion. I just wanted to do something different and unique. I wanted to be seen as a performance artist in a new way.

I WANTED TO
BE BRUCE LEE,
SO I STUDIED
MARTIAL ARTS
FOR YEARS.

"Christopher didn't grow up like a normal kid. **He worked every waking minute** of his life and his career—even as a kid. He has a tunnel vision, a goal, a passion, and a dream that he chose to dedicate his life to at a very early age. I think that's why he's so successful. **He never let anything stand in his way.**"

J. D., my brother

I fantasized about fame all the time. I usually found myself staring out the window of our family van, imagining myself on all of the billboards that dotted the sides of the Long Island Expressway. I daydreamed it was me up there in the Calvin Klein or Coca-Cola ad. I'd imagine my face on the body of the models. I tried to feel what it was like to have thousands of people stare at a billboard with my image on it. I think a lot of people fantasize about becoming a celebrity. It seemed cool and exciting to live like a rock star. From the outside, it appears as though the world is at your disposal. Who hasn't thought about being famous at one time or another?

When I was twelve years old, I began competing in the "Most Talented Kid" contests all along the eastern seaboard. I usually entered in two different categories. The first was doing a short magic routine, and the second was playing drums. I usually placed in the top three, and every now and then, I was even lucky enough to win. These events were always family outings. My mom, dad, and brothers all piled into my dad's van and drove wherever the contest was, and they'd watch me entertain the crowd doing my silly magic tricks or playing a drum solo. Wherever one of us went, we all went. We traveled together as a family then as we do now.

As a teenager, I also daydreamed I was a stuntman in the movies. I was always attempting to re-create some spectacular feat I saw on the big screen. I was certain I could do them. I would imagine myself free-falling from the roof of our house or jumping my motor cross bike over pylons and cones, and then I'd actually go out and try it. I was constantly challenging myself, putting myself through intense physical tasks. I'd climb to the roof of our house and do something stupid, like jump off, falling ten plus feet into the hedges. My father yelled at me to stop because I was ruining the hedges. Funny, he was more concerned about his disfigured bushes that he ever was about my getting hurt. Looking back, my parents never really worried about my getting hurt. Somehow, they unconditionally accepted my crazy attempts as being normal and age-appropriate.

I could not have been more blessed than to have the love and support of my family throughout the years. I would drive whoever was home absolutely crazy practicing my tricks for them. In fact, there were times my attempts were so outrageous, I can't believe my parents didn't insist on my giving up magic for good. When I was sixteen, my parents went on vacation, leaving me and my brothers home with nothing to do but practice my art. I was preparing to go to Europe to do a show. I had the house to myself and no one to tell me that what I was about to do … was nuts. I decided the living room was a perfect space for practicing the pyrotechnics for a particular demonstration. I moved all of the living room furniture into the dining room so I could have more room to practice. All of our neighbors thought we were moving because they saw the furniture piled high through the dining room windows. I set up a video camera in the corner of the room so I could later review and critique my performance. Suddenly, the carpet caught fire. That was not supposed to happen. I freaked out, especially knowing my mom wasn't going to be very happy with the outcome of this "stunt." Did I mention Mom had just finished a complete remodel? It was a dumb thing to do. I certainly knew I shouldn't be playing with fire in the house.

Years later, my parents were away again, this time on a month-long vacation in Greece visiting my mother's family. They called home to see how everything was going. I told them I was fine and suggested they enjoy themselves—stay a little longer. A week later, my parents called home again.

"How are you, Christopher?"

"Mom, Dad, I'm great. You should stay in Greece. Enjoy being there with family."

A week later I received another phone call. Again, I encouraged them to extend their stay.

This time my mother said, "Why don't you want us to come home?"

I did want them to come home, but I was afraid to tell them I had once again emptied out the living room so I could build multiple char-

BUILDING THE TRONIK PROTOTYPE IN MOM AND DAD'S BACKYARD
FOR THE *Science of Magic* SPECIAL.

acters for an upcoming television appearance. The characters took up
the entire living room, dining room, patio, and backyard! I was painting, fabricating, and building these incredible creatures.

My parents never got angry with me for pursuing my passion. They
knew I was following my dream. They did whatever they could to support me. To be certain, my ideas were grand, and none of my friends
were tempting fate on a daily basis like I was. What set me apart from
the rest of the pack was my process in planning out and executing demonstrations. Whenever I thought of an idea, I mapped it out, set it up,
and tested the possibilities until I knew I would achieve success; then I
practiced it, and finally performed it as if it were a live show. The pyrotechnics was a great example of why I needed to test everything. You
never know when something can or will go wrong.

If I was creating a jump sequence on my bike, I'd set up cones as an
obstacle course and practice weaving my bike in and out between each
one. In my mind, I was in a race, and I was out to win. I always emerged

victorious—if only in my imagination. If I were riding my motor cross bike, I'd pop wheelies and ride on the back tire. I was a bit of a show-off—sometimes too much. My cousins Gus and George and I used to go to the local school yard and practice jumping our dirt bikes over things. One particular night, as I attempted the grand finale jump, I didn't see the bench that was directly in my landing path. It was getting dark and the three of us had become a little careless and cocky. (I'm sure there were some pretty girls around we were trying to impress!) I crashed straight into the bench. The impact sent me flying twenty-five feet in the air.

I twisted my ankle really badly, but was afraid to tell my parents because I didn't want my bike taken away. I pretended I wasn't in pain for weeks. Though I wasn't consciously aware of it at the time, clearly these were early signs of developing and strengthening my pain threshold, which is essential to most everything I do today.

I've always been able to endure a higher level of pain than anyone I've ever known. The Marines say that "pain is weakness leaving the body." I never wanted to be perceived as weak so I always accepted pain as part of the learning process. Because of my endurance and ability to take high levels of pain and anxiety, I always tell people I'd be a good contender for *Fear Factor*—except for the eating part.

Ever since I was a little boy, I have been a very picky eater. When my parents told me to eat my vegetables, I'd have to sit at the table and play little tricks with my mind to get each morsel down. Coming from a large Greek family, there were frequent family dinners with colossal portions of Greek food—most of which I don't like. My father would make me sit at the table until I finished. I tried every trick to get out of it, but the only way I would be excused from the table was to eat. I practiced getting myself into a certain mind-set to get the food down without tasting it. I'd play little games with myself, like pretending I was eating something I loved. My taste in food is pretty basic. I like pizza and steak, and I am a junk food addict. It's a good thing I work out as often as I do or I'd never be able to participate in the physical aspects of my work.

TIME MISSPENT
AS A YOUTH
TRYING TO
CREATE THE
IMAGE THAT I
WAS SMALLER.

Aside from practicing stunts and magic, I spent much of my child-hood trying to figure out ways to change my appearance. It wasn't that I didn't like the way I looked, I just wanted to see if I could change the way people saw me. I'd create my own prosthetics in an attempt to make myself look like a small person. For some reason, I was obsessed with looking small. I'd roll my pants up, put my shoes on my knees, and "walk" around looking a foot shorter than I really was. I was always creating illusions that manipulated size and depth perception, skills that came in very handy as I became more adept at creating larger-scale illusions for my art and performances.

I was always desirous of doing unusual things beyond my abilities for my age. When I was twelve years old, I used to go to work at my father's coffee shop on Saturdays. I hated working there. I went because my fa-ther let me drive his huge brown Cadillac in the parking lot for twenty minutes or so after he closed for the day. I loved that he let me drive it all by myself. None of my friends' fathers let them drive. I felt totally cool.

AT FOURTEEN, I MADE MY MOM FLOAT IN THE DEN.

I get a lot of letters from kids who write to me about how their parents don't understand them or just can't relate to their interests in alternative music or expressing themselves through the way they dress or wear their hair. Parents want their kids to conform to the way society thinks they should act, look, and be. I was so fortunate to have a mom and dad who never judged me or put me down because I was different. They encouraged me to be who I am, and that support helped me grow into my own person. All I can say is that I am incredibly grateful for their wisdom. It has shaped me into the man I am today.

My dad was 100 percent Greek, but was first-generation American, born in the United States in 1937. Mom was born in Greece and came to America in 1948 at the age of thirteen. My parents had the type of relationship I have always admired. They had a wonderful life together. They're two of the most loving and selfless people I have ever known. They lived to give and never wanted anything in return. It was a priority to spend as much time together as we could, especially when my brothers and I were younger. To be honest, it's still a priority for my mom, who is now at a certain age where life should be all about her. God bless her. She still supports my every move.

I once told my mom if I wasn't a millionaire by the time I was eighteen, I'd give up magic. Well, I didn't reach that particular goal, but Mom encouraged me to keep *moving* forward and *reaching* for the stars anyway. That's her satisfaction. Whether she wanted to be or not, Mom was usually the lucky recipient of my first try at a trick. She'd drive me to the local magic shop once a week, where I'd spend my entire weekly allowance earned from doing chores around the house. There were no free rides in our house. You earned everything. I took my five-dollar weekly allowance, bought a trick, came home, and drove everyone in my family crazy.

"Hey, watch this."

I wanted their attention. They wanted to watch TV.

So I'd go to my aunt's house, which was near our home. She showed me my first trick, so she was always game for seeing what I was up to next.

"Hey, watch this."

It was an endless cycle.

"I remember coming home TO FIND
CHRISTOPHER floating my mom on a broomstick
in the living room. He was around **fourteen years old**.
I knew that day he was going to be so successful.
I was blown away by it."

J. D., my brother

39

My father awoke at four o'clock in the morning to go to work. He'd come home at seven o'clock in the evening, completely exhausted; but despite his fatigue, he always made time for his family. He instilled values like respect and trust in all of us that guide me throughout each and every day. My brothers, J. D. and Costa, feel the same way. We are a close-knit family who'd do anything for one another.

Today, both of my brothers work on my television show, and they help me run the day-to-day operation of Angel Productions. J. D.'s role is to be there for everyone. He is our rock. He also handles worldwide merchandising for all Criss Angel products. Costa helps in any way he can. He has played characters onstage with me, he has acted as part of the cast on the television show, and he is getting involved in producing. I could never do what I do without their undying and unconditional love and support. We've always been like the three musketeers. When we were kids, my brothers and I formed a band. I got my first drum set when I was six years old and have played ever since. Playing in a band can be expensive; we had to support our hobby by coming up with innovative ways to buy our equipment—instruments, amplifiers, microphones, and so on. To meet our needs, my father started a home business where we bought and sold used musical instruments. He wanted us to earn extra money and to teach us how to run a business. We'd advertise, have people come over, and one of us would sell them a used drum kit or guitar. We were constantly buying used equipment and flipping it for a profit. That business grew into a well-known music store in Levittown, New York, called Monster Music. I actually named the store and designed their logo. I thought it was a cool-sounding name.

These skills later came in very handy as a budding businessman, entrepreneur, and performer. I also learned how to deal with people and overcome their opposition in buying from me. That taught me to never take no for an answer.

To gain experience performing, I did a lot of parties in the neighborhood for free. I always enjoyed performing in front of a crowd. I

CRISS ANGEL
MINDFREAK

landed my first paid appearance as a magician at age twelve, when I performed at a neighbor's birthday party. She paid me ten dollars—twice my weekly allowance. The tricks were so bad. I was horrible. Let's just say none of those tricks are part of my current show (and you won't find any of them in the MINDFREAK section of this book either).

"I don't think *Christopher* was ever really intimidated by groups of people or by performing in front of an audience. He used to do shows at teen discotheques PERFORMING LIVE IN FRONT OF HUNDREDS OF KIDS. He got a *tremendous amount of confidence* as a kid from his parents and brothers. PERFORMING WAS INGRAINED IN HIM since the very beginning. It's **where his joy is** and has always been."

George, my cousin

In the early days, my whole family helped as much as they could. My parents, brothers, aunts, uncles, cousins, all my friends at school—everyone endured my constant barrage of practicing my next big feat. Every day was a chance to hone my skill and sharpen my craft. It was (and still is) a daily practice. I never enjoyed doing kids 'magic, though I still can do some fierce balloon characters if asked. I was a teenager dying to do adult magic. At age fourteen, I finally graduated from doing kids' parties to working Friday nights doing magic at a nearby Long Island wine bar and restaurant called the Wine Gallery. It was the kind of place couples went to on a first date. Since this was before I could drive, I had to ride my bike to work. I performed for tips only—no

pay. I was the guy who walked up to people's tables, usually inter-
rupting the first-date small talk, and asked if I could do a few tricks.
Sometimes I was a welcome distraction. Other times I think the guys
paid me to just go away. I spent three to four hours one night a week
and could easily clear a hundred dollars on a good night. At the time,
that was a lot of money to me. Bars and clubs were great venues when
I was a kid because they were so lucrative. I made a lot more money
doing magic than my buddies were making bagging groceries after
school. It's funny, because I would never have been allowed into those
establishments as a patron because I was underage, yet I could perform
there without any problems.

I spent most of my days in high school doodling and dreaming of my next trick. That's what got me through the day. I'd watch the clock tick, tick, tick away until the last bell, which allowed me to go home to build my elaborate concoctions. On weekends I had a job at a local pub. Any money I earned went to seeing new magicians and some new trick at the local magic shop. I was in constant pursuit of getting better and more sophisticated with my performances.

"Criss always had **sketchbooks for his ideas,** so he was *always creating.* I saw the tricks that he is doing on the show today in the sketchbooks years ago. They were ideas that he had drawn up in pencil, and even then HE HAD CONFIDENCE IN THEM. He would draw it out and say, 'I am going to have a giant circular saw cut me in half without a box.' I would say, 'Well, how in the hell are you going to do that?' And he would say, 'I can DO IT.' And now I just saw him do it on the show."

Mike Russo, childhood friend

I never saw myself doing anything but entertaining people. I wasn't swayed by all of the "no" people—and there were many along the way. Instead, I used them to grow, to try harder, and to become bigger and better than any magician in our time. Despite my promise to my mom, I was not a millionaire by the time I was eighteen. In fact, I was flat broke. But by then, my parents knew that college was not in my future. I graduated high school early to begin performing in Europe. They told me how important it was to get a college education, but my education would be learned on the road. It was a practical education, not a formal one.

I inherited my work ethic from my dad. He worked his entire life and was busy until the day he died. Dad owned several restaurants and doughnut shops. He built the business with his brother-in-law. They owned coffee shops in industrial areas where there were lots of factories. They became very successful revitalizing failing businesses and then flipping them for a profit. My father used to tell me how important it was to know any business from the ground up. He always made me start at the bottom—washing dishes, mopping floors, and scrubbing the toilets. As I got older, I began to bus, wait tables, cook, and sometimes work as the cashier. He'd say, "Christopher, in order to be successful in any business, you have to do every job so you can understand what is involved at every level. That's how you become a good boss, a good business owner, and a good manager."

I have taken his philosophy and advice and used it throughout my career. I have such an ambitious appetite to do big things, but I never had the budget to go along with my hunger for success, so I often found myself doing every job imaginable to get a show up and running. I had to make a dollar look like three. I'm a good magician, but that trick was tough to pull off. As a performer, I've done things onstage most people would never imagine in a million years, but the most surprising feats are the ones that happen offstage, behind the scenes. When I did my television special *Supernatural* we were short staff, so after having to perform, direct, and produce, I would also have to load up the truck after a fifty-three-hour-day. To top it off, I was the guy driving the truck, unloading the props, doing the illusions, and creating and building sets.

"*We spent years trying* to get someone to back Criss's show. He never once let any particular deal that fell through set him back. **His determination**

was amazing. **He was relentless.** He would build the sets, *build the illusions,* perform the stunts, work with the tech people. He never slept and would be **working around the clock**."

—*Peter Thea, senior VP,*
The Zomba Label Group

You name it, I was willing to do anything and everything. I was the man under the baseball cap and dark sunglasses passing out flyers promoting *MINDFREAK,* my 2001 off-Broadway show. It didn't matter. I had an insane commitment. No job was too small or daunting to distract my attention from the big picture, even the odd jobs like duct-taping floors or sweeping the stage—anything that needed to be done to get the show on the road.

Every challenge was a learning experience. I said yes to every opportunity to hone my craft and build my name and reputation. It didn't matter if it was Sunday at church, at local firehouses, Christmas parties, birthday parties, weddings, bar mitzvahs, or after school for my friends. I performed anyplace, anytime. I was like an athlete who has to keep playing to get better—except my sports of choice were magic and music.

As hard as I worked performing, I discovered it took equally intense commitment to promote myself as a performer. Even if you're the best magician or musician, when people don't know about you, you're not working. I had to get the word out, so when I wasn't performing, I was promoting. In the early days, I booked all of my own gigs. I called people every day looking for work. When I wasn't busy making phone calls to get work, I was out making the rounds to all of the local clubs in Long Island asking them if I could emcee a night of comedy and magic. I promised to fill the room in exchange for a few dollars and a percentage of the door. I hired people I knew who were entertaining—other magicians, singers, bands, whatever I could scrounge together—and I put on a show. I would agree to do shows even if I didn't know how to do what they were asking me to do. I tried doing comedy magic, serious magic, close-up magic, and any other form of magic people asked for. If I didn't know how to do something, I'd do my research on who was the best and have them help me figure it out.

I chased booking agencies, managers, and agents. They'd tell me to put together a press kit or a demo reel. What was that? How did I get a demo reel and what exactly goes into a press kit? I'd have to figure it out and make it happen. I had no money, so hiring other people to do this for me was not yet an option. Publicists and managers were still a few years down the road, so I had to be a one-stop shop where I did my own PR, cut my deals, collected my fees, and got myself work. To build my press kit, I called local newspapers and magazines to pitch them on writing articles about me. I tried to get the local news to cover my performances and developed my own cable access show called *Hot Kix*. I even found a way to get my story told on *A Current Affair*. I was relentless.

My business was beginning to grow at a fairly steady pace. People were starting to call me for events and bookings. Even though I was regularly working, I still wasn't making a lot of money. I spent every dollar I took in on creating new ways to continue building my career. In 1989 my father and I started Angel Productions, Inc. It was a money-losing venture for years. The government considered the company a "hobby" because of the continuous losses. In the mid–1990s we finally began to break even. My father told his brothers, his friends, his coworkers—everyone he talked to—that he knew I would someday make it big. Bless his soul. He believed in me so much. Any little thing I did, whether a small newspaper interview or a local showcase advertisement, Dad showed it off like I had won a Grammy Award. He was so proud of me. I could never have continued on this path without his faith.

For most magicians, Halloween is a sacred time of year. To me, it's not just a holiday, it is the anniversary of the death of one of my greatest

Illusionist Extraordinary

CHRIS SARANTAS, Illusionist
Acts Tailored for Occasions
From Levitating a Woman and Vanishing Her
To Vanishing a Rabbit

Rates by Occasion
Call CHRIS SARANTAS

FROM STAGE ACTS
TO PRIVATE PARTIES

ONE OF
MY FIRST
BUSINESS
CARDS.

inspirations, Harry Houdini. For a few years, Madison Square Garden, the arena most famous for being the home of the New York Knicks and Rangers, was converted into *Madison Scare Garden*, a giant horror show/fun house for Halloween. I was antsy to break out of my routine of performing in the clubs and bars around New York and Long Island and eager to take my career to the next level. I needed a venue to showcase myself, but I was lacking the money to stage my own show, so this kind of event was a perfect opportunity to get in front of a lot of important people. I decided to approach Lynton V. Harris, executive producer of *Madison Scare Garden* with an idea to do a complete performance for the huge crowds that came pouring through his highly successful twelve-day run. Though Lynton warned me I would have to do sixty shows a day, I wasn't the least bit deterred. I thought, "No problem. I'll just make it a ten-minute act that I can reset and start again."

In my mind, all I could think of was the opportunity to perform in front of an audience and to have a venue where I could invite press and other media to see my act. I had to make it impressive. This was a golden opportunity to build my name and garner some much needed attention.

I quickly put together a very physically demanding show. My demonstration required me to vanish, reappear, and fight "Tronik," the eight-foot-tall erector-set-looking character I had created and built in

47

my parents' living room earlier that summer. I built a small makeshift theater that gave the perception my show was its own little setting in the midst of all of the other chaos going on around us. People really responded positively to the show, especially the media. As an incentive, Lynton also agreed to let me sell my own merchandise, so I had T-shirts and baseball caps made. I set up my first Web site to market both the show and the goods. During the twelve-day run, I took in more than $50,000 in merchandise sales. That was more money than I had ever made. For the first time, people were beginning to know my name, and I had press clippings I could utilize in my portfolio. It was the beginning of what would become one of many pieces in the puzzle that make up the big picture I have held so tightly to for many, many years.

I've always known exactly where I wanted to go, and I've always been willing to do anything and everything to assure my own success. I have to admit, I was exhausted at the end of the run. This was definitely one of those things I had no idea what I was signing up for when I agreed to do sixty shows a day. Two weeks of *Madison Scare Garden* gave me a lot of practical experience before I would take on my first live show in 2001. My father taught me to take great pride in everything I do, and then be the best at whatever I choose. I never said no to opportunity. You never know where an opportunity will lead, so I always keep an open mind.

CHAPTER THREE

MIND, BODY, AND SPIRIT

ANOTHER DEMONSTRATION YEARS IN THE MAKING AND
ONE I'M THE MOST PROUD OF AS IT'S NEVER BEEN DONE
BEFORE.

For the most part, magicians are limited in the tricks they do. We can make things appear and disappear. We can move an object from one place to another. We can transform an object into something else. We can destroy an object and then restore it, and we can demonstrate something that is seemingly impossible or that defies natural laws of the universe like gravity. Finally, we can use the mind to create scenarios that appear as if we are in some way psychic or paranormal, which we are not. My philosophy on magic is simple: Think of something completely impossible and then figure out a way to do it. It's not easy, but it sure makes for great headlines.

Every book, painting, television program, song, or movie starts as a tiny seed of an idea, which is nurtured and developed by someone with the vision to see the invisible—someone who knows that it will work. Think of the impossible miracles that cell phones, television, and even the Internet offer. Without their inventors' inner vision, none of these modern-day inventions would have become reality. A magician takes the notions of science, physics, and imagination and presents them in a way that makes you, the audience, ask, "How did he do that?"

The mind has an overwhelming power to infiltrate and influence every aspect of our lives. Its potential is limitless. When the mind, body, and spirit work together and harmoniously, anything is possible. I truly believe the mind controls every aspect of the body. Your body is a slave to it. So if you're a positive thinker, your body is going to react in a positive way to any circumstance or situation. If you're a negative thinker, your body will cave to those negative thoughts. Say you feel like you're coming down with a cold or the flu. If you mentally give yourself those symptoms—aches, pains, chills, fever—you will absolutely go down hard with a bad case of whatever you imagined your body to feel. It's like that saying, you are what you eat. I believe you are what you think. What you feed your mind, your body will follow and believe. Even the most brilliant medicine in the world can't cure the body if the patient's mind refuses to cooperate.

The brain is often mistakenly seen as a separate entity from the body. To most people, the brain is a mystery. It is the place we hide our private thoughts and emotions and where we keep them safely tucked away from other people. Believing in the power of our mind requires a belief in that which we cannot see—faith or spirit. Everyone has the ability to strengthen the power of their mind. There's no pill or secret revelation. The more you understand about yourself, the closer you will come to tapping into your own resources to strengthen your mind, your body, and your spirit.

As a young, budding amateur magician, I began to grow more curious about the connections among the mind, body, and spirit. How many times have you been in a bad mood and one song on the radio turns your day around? If music can bring levity to a difficult situation, then surely an act of impossibility can do the same.

Since the mind plays such a large part in most of the demonstrations I perform, it makes sense that I needed to study how it functions to make myself an even better performer. There are mechanisms every good magician triggers to distract your attention to achieve the goal of making you believe you've just witnessed an act of magic. In great part, I ask that you suspend your preconceived ideas of what is real or possible and open your thoughts to the surreal and impossible.

One of the most dangerous demonstrations in the first season of *MINDFREAK* was the episode that showed me leaning over the roof of the fifty-first-floor Aladdin Hotel in Las Vegas, stretched out at a forty-five-degree angle, fighting extreme conditions of high winds and possible vertigo. Upping the ante even further, I commenced to walk down the side of the building without any wires, harness, or safety net, defying the law of gravity. Impossible? Thousands of people watched me do it.

What makes our eyes see something appear as real, even though we know it defies basic laws of probability, gravity, and nature? The mind cannot distinguish between a real or an imagined event. Therefore, everything you see is open to interpretation: Was it real or an illusion?

There have been plenty of times in my career when my mind tried to tell my body that what I was doing wasn't natural. It defied what my mind knows to be logical, safe, secure, and reasonable. This mind-body connection has been talked about a lot by many people in various fields. When I talk about it, it takes on a whole new dimension. I am in situations on a daily basis that are beyond most people's realm and concept of reality. There is simply no room for negativity when I am performing. I can't allow myself to think morbid thoughts. If I do, those thoughts can run amok. I have to be very conscientious about controlling them or they will infiltrate my entire being and have the opposite effect I need to complete a demonstration.

We've all had bad thoughts about what might happen, things that could go terribly wrong. Maybe it's the night before a big trip, and you worry about or contemplate the idea that the plane might crash or that you're going to be in a horrible accident. At one time or another, we've all played a morbid game of "what if."

When I did my first television special, also called MINDFREAK, I did a demonstration where I had placed two coins over my eyes, duct-taped them shut, and put on a blindfold, then walked up the side of a water tower, two hundred feet in the air. There were no safety lines, no cushion below if I fell. I walked two I-beams that were two inches wide and were separated in the middle by a space that was no more than eight inches. I placed my feet on each of them and walked around the span of the water tower. When I began the demonstration, my legs felt like lead—it felt like each weighed a thousand pounds. My mind was telling my body, this is wrong. It was definitely something I should not have been doing, yet I pushed myself to move through each baby step I took. The danger factor was very real and considerably extreme. If I had taken one wrong step, I would have wiped out, falling two hundred feet—it would have been the end. In hindsight, I know it was extremely

BLIND-FOLDED AND MORE THAN TWO HUNDRED FEET ABOVE THE GROUND, DURING MY *Supernatural* TV SPECIAL.

foolish to take that kind of risk, but it was my first television special, and I felt I needed to push the limits because I had something to prove. This was a few years ago, a time when I had no cash and a need to show the world what magic can be, Criss Angel style.

I was compelled to call upon my entire being, my mind, body, and spirit to work as one. When they all come together, there's an indescribable sense of positive energy and an overwhelming desire to accomplish whatever you set out to do—even if it means risking your life. When it happens, it's downright spiritual. I felt complete. In fact, I was strangely at peace. If something were to go wrong, it would've been okay. I was

PREPARING
FOR OASIS.

in a moment of unconditional acceptance. The outcome doesn't matter. Those are the moments I live for.

If the mind, body, and spirit are not in top form, you will never be in top form. That is when people get hurt. If I am not physically ready for a demonstration, I know I will not be able to accomplish the technical aspects that are required. If I am carrying emotional baggage around, I have to clear my mind of whatever that baggage is and focus on whatever I need to do to get through the task at hand. I have to mentally shove that stuff right out of my head. For me, it's usually a matter of life or death. Anyone who has ever worked around me before I attempt a particularly dangerous demonstration knows I'm in an extremely focused state. This is not an ideal time to try and talk to me. When I'm in the zone, I don't want to hear anything but my own thoughts. It's critical for me to be in the right place, in the right state of mind.

When I am not connected, it's a recipe for disaster. Toward the end of the first season filming *MINDFREAK*, I did a demonstration called Oasis, which took five years to work through from inception to demonstration. Even though I was very tired and pretty burned-out, I had waited so long to do it. I'd been operating on three hours of sleep a night. That's all I usually need to get by. But after the crazy schedule we had been on I was really beat. I felt like a prizefighter who didn't have the ability to train like I once did for the big fight, and who goes into the ring as champion but is clearly not at the top of his game. I decided to go through with the demonstration, but I risked my life doing it.

Oasis placed me in a completely airtight isolation chamber, which was just big enough to contain me in both height and circumference, for twenty-four hours. The chamber was then completely submerged in thousands of gallons of water so people could view all angles 360 degrees around it. If my isolation chamber had sprung the slightest little leak, water would have rushed in and instantly crushed me to death. I led people to believe it was going to be a basic escape. Instead, I actually

AMUSING MYSELF IN MY EIGHTEENTH HOUR IN OASIS.

JUST ABOUT TO HOLD MY BREATH AS I GET LOCKED INTO
THE WINE BARREL.

In 2002, I submerged myself in water for twenty-four hours in the middle of Times Square on *Good Morning America*.

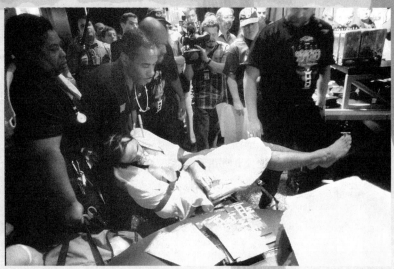

vanished from inside the isolation chamber after twenty-four hours. People looking into the tank saw that I had disappeared before their eyes. They heard me scream as I reappeared across the park, and were completely blown away.

To get through Oasis, I drew upon the experience of my demonstration Submerged, which I did in 2002. Submerged was my tribute to Houdini's famous escape from a water torture cell for my first television special. Houdini often performed his Chinese Water Torture Cell twice a night over the course of thirteen years during his career. He was locked in a tank of water and was surrounded by a curtained cabinet. His audience waited patiently, calculating how long they could hold their own breath. Sometimes Houdini escaped in as little as thirty seconds. Sometimes he extended the suspense, taking more than two minutes before revealing he had escaped. The longer it took Houdini to appear, the more uncomfortable the crowd would grow. Houdini waited for the anxiety level to reach a feverish pitch before bursting through the curtain, dripping with water and gasping for air. The dramatic effect was enormous. Houdini had an uncanny ability to calculate the right moment for the biggest impact.

My version of Submerged began as an idea I had while taking a shower. Like Houdini, I encapsulated myself in a water-filled container that was built exactly to the specifications of my body. I couldn't hear—my ears were constantly popping from the pressure. I was sleep-deprived. I couldn't eat and couldn't see. I couldn't use the bathroom, so I had depleted my body of fluids and waste before attempting this stunt. My loss of senses was intense. It physically affected other parts of my body. I developed a severe headache from the built-up pressure, and I had a very difficult time regulating my body temperature, going back and forth from shivering cold to blazing hot. I have a scar under my nose from the mask I wore; it rubbed against my skin, which became very raw and tender from the water. The human body is not meant to be in that kind of isolation for any period of time, let alone twenty-four hours. I was handcuffed and shackled. I was completely submerged in water. Spectators could see my every move until the water filtration system failed, which caused the water to become murky, almost milky white, from my own skin cells' shedding and my body oils' being depleted. It was incredibly challenging, but I did it. After twenty-four hours, in New York's Times Square I escaped from the water chamber, alive and exhausted.

"When Christopher made his escape, he was **high from the adrenaline**. He did a television interview and then walked twenty feet outside to *thank the fans* and media. He came back inside, took two steps, and collapsed in my arms. It was **terrifying** and emotionally draining."

J. D., my brother

When planning Submerged, I knew I wanted to do something that took Houdini's concept further than anyone had ever done; whereas in Oasis, I wanted to psychologically set people up to see me in what would be an impossible escape scenario and never fathom that I could vanish and instantaneously reappear someplace else. Oasis was an illusion. Submerged was an escape. I had to be able to do Submerged to successfully pull off Oasis. I knew it wouldn't be easy since I had spent twenty-four hours in the hospital after completing Submerged.

I'm not afraid to put it all on the line for the sake of my art. No one takes the types of chances I take as a performer or a magician. If something doesn't work, it can put me out of business. People fear embarrassment, and they certainly fear failure.

The only other time I wasn't connected to a demonstration, I actually chose to cancel it. I was scheduled to jump off the garage of the Aladdin Hotel, do a free fall, and catch a playing card out of a deck that was going to be thrown in the air as I jumped. I didn't feel like I had enough time to do the due diligence in training. I hadn't had the opportunity to work with a trainer to perfect the free fall, and my gut told me this was wrong. My mind and body were definitely disconnected on this one. It was a greater risk than I needed to take in order to do a card trick. I've never been the type of guy who accepted defeat or gave in to failure. After thinking about other possibilities to do the trick, I came up with the idea of riding my motorcycle in place of the free fall. Same trick, same effect. Problem solved.

I had someone select a card out of a deck. I asked them to sign it, put it in the back of the deck, and hold on to the deck. I got on my chopper, rode away, and told them to throw the deck up in the air in front of me as I came back and rode through the crowd. I showed everyone that my hands were empty—no gimmicks. I was going to pluck that person's card out of the air as the cards were falling down and I drove by. To everyone's shock and delight, I did just that. It looked amazing, and I believe the demonstration ended up being better than the free fall would have been for the episode.

Like so many things in my life, something that was supposed to happen didn't come to fruition. I thank God for that. I've learned to roll with the punches and I always end up in a much better place than I would have been in if my original plans had worked out. Sometimes you have to let a situation play out. Look at it, study it, analyze it, and learn from it. Make it work for you. Use it to your advantage. My mom always told me, "If it's meant to be, it's meant to be. If it's not, it'll never happen. Don't worry about it." Those words have served me well over the years, but the truth is, I still obsess.

My ego is never satisfied. I want to always be better at what I do. To me, there's always something wrong with what I do, or some area that could stand a little improvement. I'm a perfectionist. I might like a particular demonstration one week, and hate it the next. I am always striving to be the very best I can be, which is a total circle jerk for someone like myself, since I know I can always be better. Perfection is impossible, so the pursuit of perfection is a constant, never ending, and infinite chase.

CHAPTER FOUR

MY DAD

I OFTEN REMINISCE ABOUT THE GOOD OL' TIMES—ME
AND MY DAD SITTING ON MY BROTHER'S BARRACUDA.

As you can probably tell by now, I come from a family where we genuinely care about one another. In some ways, I know what we have as a family is rare. We are tight and committed to seeing one another do well. There's unconditional love and support that I recognize as being an essential ingredient in my own success. I am who I am today because of my father's guidance and sage wisdom. He lived an authentic life. He is my inspiration to try to live up to the standard to which he lived his life. He set the bar pretty high. I strive each day to make him proud.

My dad was a pretty strict disciplinarian. It was my mom who always tried to coax Dad into loosening the reins. I wasn't even allowed to wear blue jeans as a kid! I could never sneak out of the house in the middle of the night or get away with smoking a cigarette. Someone was always looking over my shoulder, whether it was one of my older brothers or my parents. I guess that comes with being the baby of the family. Despite the strict rules, I managed to keep everyone on their toes. I wasn't a bad kid, but I was always pushing limits.

In 1995 my father was diagnosed with stomach cancer. After he heard the news, the doctors delivered a second blow. The disease had progressed to stage four—the worst-case scenario. Doctors gave him three weeks to live. Dad was the type of man who didn't buy into what the doctors were telling him. He knew he could outlive their grim prediction. As the saying goes, that which does not kill you, makes you stronger. At least for my dad, it inspired him to live stronger. He started doing sit-ups and push-ups every morning just to prove he was a man of strength. He was very ill on the inside, but on the outside his physical condition was superb.

For most of his life, Dad was always the picture of strength and good health. He understood the science of nutrition and physical activity, even before it became fashionable. As a young man, he was a body builder featured in many muscle magazines. He was a Golden Gloves boxing champ and a Pennsylvania state wrestling champion. His

MY MOM AND DAD.

SKINNY...

want a big powerful AND muscular body?

ASKS BARTON HORVATH

● If you're sick and tired with your 'skin and bones' body and want to trade it in for muscular perfection, but don't know how to go about building up your body, then this article is tailor-made for you. In it you will learn exactly what equipment is best to make you a muscular he-man, or—if you already have a set of weights but no courses to follow, then this article will start you off right.

GETTING started in bodybuilding is always the hardest part, and the most important as well!

For, if you fall into bad exercise habits early in your career or if you buy equipment which is not best for your purpose you will waste time, effort and even money and not get as far as you should in the game.

Therefore, in this article we will explain the fundamental facts about bodybuilding which will help beginners to select the correct equipment and to get started on the right foot.

First, let us tackle the problem of the beginner who wants to start training as soon as possible, but who doesn't know exactly what equipment he needs. He sees all the ads in the magazine, becomes confused and delays in making his purchase. In this way he wastes time; time that could be used to overcoming his physical inferiority, and even when he does decide to send in an order, there is some chance that he will make the wrong choice.

Just what you need to start training depends on two things. 1—your age. 2—how far you want to go in the sport.

Let's consider age first and your physical goal after that.

Young fellows under 15 years of age who are of average size and strength will do best in ordering our 105 pound dumbbell, bar-

A short time ago, powerful John Santos was a typical underdeveloped beginner. Now, after a short while of training he holds the title of Jr. Mr. Lehigh Valley, and he's only 17 years old! If you are a skinny beginner and want muscles like his, then read this article right now. —VULCAN.

18

athleticism and physique were always important to him. He had the chance to play football on scholarship for Penn State but chose to take care of his parents instead of attending college. Family was everything to my dad.

He was such a strong man in both character and physical strength. Throughout his life and during his illness, he continued to train like an elite athlete. I think that kept him alive much longer than anyone expected. Remarkably, the day after the cancer surgery on his stomach, Dad got up from his hospital bed and began walking so he could quickly rebuild his strength. He always had such a positive outlook. Dad had a marvelous attitude about connecting the mind, body, and spirit, something that was very forward-thinking for the time. I watched him and marveled at his attempts to conquer the disease that was eating away at his life. I absorbed his spirit into mine. He amazed me each and every day.

There were some really rough days during my father's illness, but he always smiled. He lit up a room. When anyone asked how he was doing, Dad would always answer, "I'm doing great." Other people talked to him about their personal issues, and instead of thinking of himself, he reached out to help by talking to them and motivating them to change their circumstances. He tried to live the final years, months, weeks, and days of his life as if nothing were wrong. He never once gave in to the notion of his mortality. He never complained about pain or discomfort. His motivation was simple; he had a grandchild on the way. At the time, my brother J. D. and his wife were expecting a baby. My father was determined to live long enough to meet his first grandchild. And he did.

My father used to say, "Illness is a part of life, son." He taught me to appreciate the people you love and to cherish each moment because you don't know how many moments you're going to have. I think about those words every day—especially those days I am putting my life on the line by choice. My father didn't have a choice about dying. His disease was irreversible. He had to live knowing he could die at any given moment. That's why I don't fear death. I don't worry about dying at all. Death is a great stimulus for the imagination. I watched my father live a peaceful life, even in his final moments. Our family is very spiritual, but my father was an extremely religious man. He had faith and believed you can move mountains if you set your mind to it. If you have enough belief in yourself, there's nothing you can't do—especially when you're willing to work for it. His faith gave my dad comfort that allowed him to cope and deal with his failing health.

Watching my father die was agonizing for me. It made me take a step back and assess my choices in life. Let's face it. Everybody is dealt a different hand in life. It's all about how we choose to play that hand. Some people die in their sleep, others get hit by a car, while others attempt death-defying stunts that sometimes, not often, but sometimes can go very, very wrong. Choices. Life is full of choices.

"Even though my dad is no longer with us, there's a little bit of him that lives inside my brothers and me. We all have something from him that he's given to us. *We were blessed* to have had him. If we can be **a fraction of the man** that he was, that's something to strive for. If we can do that, we will have lived a **successful and fulfilling life**."

Costa, my brother

When my father was diagnosed, I put my career on hold. I wanted to stay at home and take care of him. I had a harder time accepting my father's fate than he did. When his throat became too blocked to eat or drink, I made sure he had fluids by hand-feeding him water and juice using a teaspoon. I became desperate to get him the help he needed to survive. Every doctor we took him to said the same thing: "There's nothing we can do." I can't accept that self-defeatist attitude, not for me, and certainly not when it came to my father's life. There must have been something we could do. I make my living figuring out ways to make the impossible possible. Surely I could find a solution to this problem. I insisted the doctors perform a tracheotomy so my father could breathe on his own a little easier. Maybe it was selfish, but I wanted as much time as I could get with him.

Still, it was hard for me to accept, but my father was fading away. I realized it was more important to choose how we would spend our last moments together than it was to find a way to prolong the inevitable.

My father died in 1998. He died in my arms. I knew he was strug-

MY DAD POSING WITH TRONIK, JUST BEFORE HE WAS DIAGNOSED. TO THIS DAY, I TAKE THIS PICTURE WITH ME EVERYWHERE I GO.

gling to hold on, but it was time to let him go. I whispered to my father, "Go." He closed his eyes and peacefully drifted away.

My dad's death helped me realize how precious life is. My perspective on everything changed after he passed. Things I thought were important, like music or magic, paled in comparison to cancer and death. What I do is entertainment. It's not cancer. We have troops overseas fighting a war, endangering their lives for the sake of ours, for the sake of our country. It sometimes makes it hard for me to think what I offer is in any way significant or should be rewarded. And yet bringing entertainment to the world, making people think and feel, raising their consciousness and belief that anything is possible, is relevant if not essential. Historically speaking, entertainment has always thrived in times of war and depression. People need that escape then, now, and forever. I had to press on.

My sense of responsibility to take care of my mom and the rest of my family was enormous after my father died. Although I'm the crazy one in the bunch, we all understand one another really well. We have tremendous respect, trust, and love for one another. Of course, those feelings are heightened when it comes to my mom.

As a performer, my aim is to do all kinds of wild, dangerous stunts and tricks to ensure you fully engage in my demonstration from beginning to end. To accomplish this, I am always pushing the limits of what is attainable without getting hurt. You can't be senseless when you attempt the kinds of demonstrations I do. You have to have a balanced blend of courage, training, diligence, and skill. If you don't, you will end up killing yourself or being very disappointed with the outcome.

Look, I don't want to die, but risk is a part of what I do. You can't live your life in fear. What I do is insignificant in the real world because I choose to place myself in dangerous situations. I recognize the risks I take. I don't have to. I want to. My father and other people with illness in this world don't choose to have that illness. It chooses them. My father was never scared—or at least he never let on that he was frightened in any way. He had a resolve that was enviable and admirable.

My father chose to be incredibly positive and to tap into the kind of courage I have never had to know. His inner strength and outlook on life was such an inspiration. Everything I do, I do for him. I dedicate my life, my art, my success, and my love to my father. It is my greatest disappointment that my dad isn't here to see what I'm doing. All of those years of struggling, scraping together every last dime to stage a show, all of those years of promising him I'd make it—somehow it would all seem so much more significant if Dad were still here.

Courage is a willingness to face what is not easy. Courage empowers people to be stronger, to grow and evolve as better people. Being honest with myself is my greatest act of courage. I live in a world of make-believe. A made-up fantasyland of illusion. It takes a lot of guts to look in the mirror and call yourself out, to see what and who you really are. It takes a tremendous amount of bravery to say you've been wrong. It may not be the most popular answer or what someone else wants to hear, but it takes courage to face the truth. Courage comes in all shapes, sizes, and forms. To me, my father demonstrated the type of courage where he shielded his family from his pain. He didn't want any of us, including himself, to go to a negative place. He wanted to uplift us and be an indelible role model. What amazes me is that he would wake up every day and say he felt great—even when I know he felt like shit. His outlook has given me a totally different perspective and appreciation for days when I feel sick. I always know I'll get better. My dad didn't have that luxury.

I often get a chance to meet kids with disabilities, who are in wheelchairs or whose bodies are riddled with terminal diseases. They have a smile from ear to ear. They have a love for their family and an appreciation for every minute of life. They have a disposition and acceptance of their lives that just blows my mind. They appreciate what they have and don't focus on what's missing or what they're losing. They don't get caught up in the crap most people do, myself included. Seeing these kids is a reminder of how important it is to enjoy the moment. I find myself gravitating toward challenged people because I know that at the end of the day, they live a richer life in a shorter amount of time than most of us. They totally get the difference between quality and quantity.

No one knows how long they have to live. When I'm in a wine barrel attempting to escape high above a concrete parking lot before the barrel is dropped and I am splattered all over the ground, I can tell myself, This will be over in a few minutes. I know I'll be fine and that I'll survive. I don't fear anything I do, because I don't fear death. When you don't fear death, what on earth is there to fear? It doesn't matter if I'm lying in a coffin trying to escape or lighting myself on fire, I face fear head-on—I find my courage and muster up my composure to stay cool and keep myself professional. I tell myself to just get through what I've got to do. I trust my instincts and my training to know without a doubt that I will survive. That's how I get through a lot of my performances. If I don't kill myself, I know I'll be all right.

AUG · 68 ·

J. D., DAD, COSTA, MOM, AND ME.

"Dad was *the main link in our family*. To lose
the main link of a chain means that chain is broken.
LOSING OUR DAD was such a blow to each and every
one of us. Not having him in the equation was such
an empty feeling. But IT BROUGHT US CLOSER
because we no longer had our dad.
We had to support one another."

J. D., my brother

Not long after my father passed away, I found the motivation to really get my website up and running. My first album was coming out, and I needed a place to sell it. My father always told me it was important to appear bigger than any venue I was playing. He said it was better to create the perception that you're larger-than-life, that you're more successful than you might actually be. I had set up corporate headquarters for Angel Productions in the den of my mother's home. I set up a four-line phone system that answered automatically and gave you options like, "You've reached Angel Productions Incorporated. If you want to reach Criss Angel, press 1. To reach Angel Productions Incorporated Recording Artists Group, press 2." I thought this system followed my dad's idea of appearing bigger than we were. Of course, I answered all of the calls, processed all of the credit card orders, and took messages for Criss as "Nicholas." I wanted to use a different voice when I answered as Nicholas, so that no one knew they were speaking to me. I didn't have enough money in those days to hire an actual assistant. I barely had enough money to pay the phone bill.

To sell my CD, I installed a toll-free 800 number. Occasionally, people phoned in to order the CD and I'd forget about Nicholas and answer the phone using my real voice. People would say, "Criss, is that you?" I could never say yes. One day, I started getting an inordinate number of calls—my phone was ringing off the hook. I'd answer and people were asking about booking the trip they just heard about on TV. I was getting hundreds of calls a day asking about a European vacation offer. I did a little research and discovered a European travel company was using an 800 number that was similar to mine.

Just in case you didn't know this, when you call an 800 number, the company you're calling pays for that call. All of a sudden, I was paying for hundreds of phone calls a day that had nothing to do with selling my CD. It was beginning to add up—and fast. I called the travel company to explain the situation. They were losing money and busi-

EVERY MOMENT IS BUT A MEMORY TO CHERISH FOREVER.
MY DAD AND I AT HIS SIXTIETH BIRTHDAY PARTY.

ness because I had a similar phone number. I suggested they buy the number from me. They offered me $30,000! Because of that, I was able to fund myself for the next year, allowing me to do what I needed to do to advance my career to the next level. I wanted to get out of playing small clubs and rooms and move into larger live shows.

CHAPTER FIVE

ILLUSIONS, REALITY, AND SURREALITY

In Two, an illusion that was inspired from the
1930s, and one I worked on for more than twelve
years and will perform to myself every night in
my live show.

My goal in creating my art is to bring something much more artistic and thematic to life than audiences have been used to seeing in the past. The idea is to combine surreal and real elements and present everything, from something that starts as an idea in my head to very personal experiences from my day-to-day life. My illusions are comprised of several pieces of a puzzle that come together and tell a story. Most of the time, the ideas are not a conscious decision. I just see things in my mind—images, people, characters, whatever. Or perhaps I'll hear a song that might inspire me to create something I know my audience will connect with. It almost doesn't matter to me how these ideas are born. If I broke it down and really analyzed every thought, every concept, every artistic expression I have, I'm certain each would reflect various areas of my own life. How I get there is less important to me than the final outcome.

I communicate through my art. What I do is merely a vehicle to convey messages to my audience that are purposely subjective and interpretive. I'm very intentional in my execution because I want people to come to their own conclusions about what they've just seen, heard, felt, sensed, and experienced. It can be emotional, exciting, nerve-racking, joyful, and exhilarating. Any response is a good response. No response means I failed to entertain, provoke thought, or move you. As a performer, I can't think of anything worse.

I like to think of myself as a student of humanity. I'm obsessed with studying people and what we, as a whole, find fascinating about one another. To me, blending a virtual world with the real world is the best way to evoke some kind of powerful response from the audience. I never want my audience to know where reality begins or ends. If I'm successful, I blur that line into obscurity. I understand human need really well. That is why I am effectively able to construct a fully encompassed experience that people like to be a part of. Sometimes my audience gets so involved they feel as if they're actually a part of the show, which is the ultimate compliment to me as both creator and performer. As emotional as I make the experience for you, I have to remain completely detached from the emotional aspects of the demonstration. My mind and focus have to stay on the task at hand, entertaining, engaging, and bewildering my audience.

"**If he can survive** being hung from fishhooks, being **burned alive**, the worst phobia you can think of . . . and *you connect to it* to enrich your own life, then that is the greatest outcome he could hope for."

J. D., my brother

When you think about it, my job is really about conquering fears. It's about doing the impossible and being the very best person I can be. It's about taking control of my destiny and being in control of all the outside elements that influence my daily life. If I lead by example, then

77

IMPALED . . . OR AM I?

perhaps you will find inspiration to do the same in your life. There are a lot of deliberate subliminal messages throughout my shows. I do this because I want you to walk away knowing *your* life can be better. Hey, if I can survive being buried alive or being submerged in a tank of water for twenty-four hours, you can take on that coworker or boss who makes your job a little harder or that teacher who pushes you to be a better student. Whatever it is in your life that challenges you, I promise, you have the strength to overcome it with a strong mind, body, and spirit. Come on. Admit it. We all need a little life resurrection from time to time.

For the most part, we each live riding the daily roller coaster of life. Some of us throw our hands up in the air and go along for the ride. Others close their eyes, grip on tight, and hold on for dear life. I want people to be on the edge of their seats when they're watching my television show or sitting in an audience during a live performance. I want them wondering if I'm going to survive my next crazy stunt

and connecting with the beauty of the illusion of floating between two buildings. They see my family biting their nails in anticipation that I'm about to kill myself because the possibility always exists that I will. Their fear is real—there are no guarantees I will survive. But then, everything's okay. Perhaps, in the final analysis, that offers you some level of comfort, even if it's just a few minutes' escape from your own daily grind. Maybe my demonstrations are a small window of opportunity to dream or fantasize about things we'd all like to do—flying, walking through fire, being a superhero. In the end, I hope my message is the same as Houdini's.

"I've been a part of almost every demonstration my son has accomplished. The one that got to me the most was Buried Alive. Attempting to do what even Houdini could not do, my son decided to be buried alive and escape death. *I cry every time* I see that episode of *MINDFREAK*. It gives me the chills. It was THE MOST REAL EXPERIENCE I HAVE EVER HAD watching my son do a demonstration. Everyone who was there began to worry that Christopher might not make it. *The Amazing Joe* was the last time SOMEONE TRIED THIS ESCAPE, and he died in his attempt. Even though he tells me not to worry, that he'll be okay, *I'm his mother*. I can't help but worry."

Dimitra, my mom

I try to send out positive messages through my work. I don't allow my imagination to take me to places where I get scared, feel alone, or am unable to overcome my fears. Negativity comes from a wrong mind-set. You have to learn to cancel out negative thoughts whenever they come along. If I start to have a negative thought, I try to have fun with it, to outsmart it. I jot it down, capture it on paper, and then recreate those scenarios in a surreal and nonthreatening way so they are no longer a deterent.

As whacked and out there as some of my stuff appears, I'd like to believe there's tremendous substance behind everything I do. It comes from a very deep place inside my soul. All of my material is filled with metaphors and interpretive messages. For example, I devoted an entire episode of *MINDFREAK* to vanishing.

Why?

Well, who hasn't wanted to disappear, escape, or vanish from their life or problems at one time or another? There are lots of days I wish

At Sunset Park in Last Vegas performing a series of levitations that I am asked about more frequently than anything I have ever done before.

I could. As a performer, I look at each demonstration I do as an opportunity to open minds, to break down barriers, and to help you connect your mind, body, and spirit in a very new and deeply meaningful way.

A lot of people ask me about the very surreal dream-nightmare sequences that appeared in the first season of *MINDFREAK*. It's a look inside my mind's eye. These thoughts are embodied in the form of abstract tableaus that reflect my subconscious thoughts. Since I usually sleep only three hours a night, I don't really have a chance to allow my mind to get into a dream state. When I do get an idea in the middle of the night, I write it down, because I know there's always some relevance—whether it's conscious or not. Since revealing my inner thoughts is just as important to me as demonstrating and performing my art, I created these short sequences to end each segment of my show leading into

THE SURREAL FAMILY PORTRAIT FROM SEASON ONE.

the commercial breaks. I interspersed vignettes using a surreal cast of characters who, in a perverse way, represent various family members and important influences in my life—real or imagined. Some people loved them, others didn't understand them. Each of the characters reflects some piece of me. I thought it would be an interesting way to open myself up to the audience so they could see the multidimensional layers and influences that make up the whole of the character you all know as Criss Angel.

All of the sequences were actually shot in the desert over a period of five days. We had a two-and-a-half-hour drive each way in and out of the desert every day. I got up between two and three o'clock in the morning to be there by six thirty and stay until sunset, when I'd jump back into the trailer, drive back to the hotel in Las Vegas, and have a production meeting about the following day before starting all over again. I always get in over my head because I'm not only acting in these scenes, I'm creating, writing, directing, and executive-producing. Somehow, I always find my way out and usually come out on top.

Everything you see is real. It was extremely important to me to perform these sequences without the use of any trick photography, use of a green screen, or special effects. Everything you see me do was shot organically. I was really in the desert being propelled out of the ground. We dug a huge hole for an air cannon in the middle of the desert. We used flash pods of fuel explosions. We buried eight different crew members next to them—each holding one of the picture frames. We literally pushed them through the desert floor on cue after I was air-cannoned through the desert floor.

All of the elements in those sequences were designed to make you think. There's something for everybody in these short snippets from my mind. There's a dual reality between my "real" and "surreal" families. The characters loosely resemble members of my family and important influences on my life. I am extremely proud of the work that we did to put these spots together. There are a lot of delicate subliminal messages throughout those vignettes. If you repeatedly watch them, you'll pick up on a subtlety that you might have missed the first time you watched it. They are deeply personal and reflective of my innermost thoughts and ideas about life, family, magic, love, and art.

Theo is the older gentleman, who represents an uncle or father figure. He's played by Johnny Thompson, who is a source of wisdom behind the scenes of my show as well. His character is older and someone to be respected. Through his actions, it is clear he has lost his mind yet still has random strokes of genius. He was a magician who perhaps knew Houdini. Theo is a compilation of several people in my life. Mostly, I see him as myself as an old man. He's an older alter ego. He has lived a full, productive life and dreams about his younger days of creative greatness.

Ginger (actually a female impersonator) is a character based on and reflective of my mother. She is loving, endearing, and generous. She is always giving and doesn't care about getting. She is the nurturer, always concerned with the family. Her heart is huge, and the warmth and generosity of her spirit emanates from her every pore.

Kayala is like the cousin Marilyn character from *The Munsters* television show. She is a pretty, exotic girl who doesn't belong in the mix. She could be a love interest or simply a cousin. I've intentionally left that up to the audience to decide.

Erich is a character I based on Houdini. Harry Houdini's real name was Erich Weiss. This character represents the spirit of Houdini, who has come back as a tweaked-out little boy.

Luigi, played by a little person actor friend, is a bodyguard character who pokes fun at what it's like for me sometimes dealing with the famous side of being Criss Angel. Even though Luigi is a little person, he is strong and tough and has my back. He's always looking out for me. He's the antithesis of what you might expect my bodyguard to look like. I wish he was really my bodyguard! I love the concept of Luigi and Criss taking on the world.

For the second season of *MINDFREAK* I added a new character, Half Animal. He's a funky, wild, crazy-looking thing that has very human mannerisms, though he is not of this world. His bottom half is animal, and his top half is human. The combination is meant to be left open to interpretation.

A&E had a difficult time with the desert sequences. Although they didn't tell me not to do the scenes, they were very skeptical of them. They didn't test well with audiences. In television, the goal is to play to your audience, but as an artist, I needed an outlet to express my inner self. These small snapshots of my inner thoughts and mind are really important to me. Still, A&E felt they distracted the viewer from the magic. I totally disagreed. They are part of the magic, of the total experience. I was trying to make something that looks like a Fellini film or a Dalí painting. The idea of me and this dysfunctional family of freaks living in the desert, surviving against the elements, and connecting as a unit, seamlessly blurring the lines between the real and imaginary

THE STORYBOARDS ARE REPRESENTATIVE OF A THOUGHT BORN IN MY HEAD, BEING SKETCHED OUT, AND THEN COMING TO FRUITION IN THE OPENING OF MY TELEVISION SHOW EVERY WEEK.

85

worlds, all seemed so much bigger than allowing a Humvee to drive over my chest as I lay on a bed of nails. I fought the network to keep them a part of the show. I'm a fighter when it comes to things I really believe in. It's part of my spirit. Fortunately A&E agreed to go with my vision, and in the end I think the show is much better for it.

CHAPTER SIX

INSPIRATIONS

AT HOUDINI'S GRAVE AT THE MASPETH
CEMETERY IN NEW YORK.

> IT'S NOT THE TRICK; IT'S THE MAGICIAN.
> — HARRY HOUDINI

When I first started practicing magic, I was

horrible onstage. I had a hard time finding my niche. I tried blending magic with my singing, but it was miserable and embarrassing. I wasn't a good enough musician at the time to do both. At first, I went for the obvious. I'd wheel out a box and cut someone in half, with a live band performing behind me, while singing! It was so cheesy. But I was relentless. I always thought magicians were hokey. I never saw myself wearing a tuxedo and pulling rabbits out of hats. I took a step back, analyzed my influences, and tried to hone in on what I could do to stand out in the crowd.

At the time, my greatest influences were MTV and music. Ozzy Osbourne, Elvis, Mötley Crüe. Those were the people I aspired to be like. I spent years trying to figure out how I could take my magic and present it in a way that would appeal to the kids who watch MTV. No one had ever done that. I saw the opportunity and opening. I began to fixate on how to combine all of the outside influences with my ideas and approach for my presentation onstage. Although I have been intrigued and influenced by several illusions and specific types of magic, Harry Houdini and Aldo Richiardi were the only two magicians who truly inspired me as an artist.

A MOMENT OF REFLECTING ON HOUDINI.

Harry Houdini was very provocative for his day. He knew exactly how to push people's buttons. Houdini had a penchant for performing many of his demonstrations wearing only a loincloth. He believed performing like this was the best way to prove to the audience he had nothing to hide. If he stood there mostly naked, his audience would have to buy into the notion that what he was doing was indeed magic. Although he wasn't considered to be a great magician, Houdini really knew how to connect with the public. As a performer, that really interested me. I knew the importance of bonding with my audience and the value of bringing them into my performance on an emotional level. From that perspective, my studies of Houdini and his techniques taught me more about performing than any other single influence.

I loved Houdini's primary message: If I can get out of this situation, you can get out of yours. People loved him for that. He was just a little guy, but he performed mighty, powerful, and unbelievable feats of great strength and skill. He was a Renaissance man whose interests were as diverse and varied as his demonstrations.

I don't think Houdini would ever have taken the risks that I take. He created the illusion that his work was dangerous. He wanted the audience to be scared and anxious. He definitely had dangerous moments, demonstrations where his life was in peril, such as when he hung upside down by his ankles several feet in the air and attempted an escape. There were lots of things that could have gone wrong, but for the most part, he controlled the escape from beginning to end, creating dramatic moments that drew audible gasps from the audience. That was part of the act. He was brilliant in building up to tense and uncertain moments, many of which I now use as parts of my own act.

Aldo Richiardi was another of my earliest influences. A Peruvian gentleman and a phenomenal performer, he had studied ballet, and at one time in his life had even worked as a matador. His movement was elegant, graceful, and dramatic. His use of music was also brilliant and something that inspired me in my own performances. When I watched him, he commanded my complete attention. I saw his show and viewed his tapes so many times, I knew his every gesture. Richiardi had an amazing skill to make his audience believe, without a doubt, that he embodied a power that drew everyone in like a magnet. When he moved a finger, your eye was captivated by it. He was mesmerizing.

My parents took me to see his show when he came to New York. At the end of the show, Richiardi always performed the same beautiful routine with his daughter Rena. He brought her onstage, placed her on a table, took a circular saw that was three feet around, and cut her in half at her midsection. Blood and guts would shoot everywhere. I could literally smell it from my seat in the audience. It appeared totally real and believable. It was a somber experience.

The illusion was very powerful. Unlike most magicians, Richiardi broke one of the pillar rules of theatrical performance: He busted the barrier between audience and performer by inviting the audience to come up onstage after the show and experience his little girl cut in half, with her blood and guts pouring out of her body. It was revolutionary to utilize both the audience and the performer during a live stage show. The impact of becoming part of the illusion was tremendous. It certainly heightened my awareness of emotionally drawing in an audience. As a premise, what could be more powerful than a father taking the life of his child? It was simply gorgeous and profound because it messed with the mind. It wasn't natural. It wasn't what a parent was supposed to do. In the end, he never even pieced his daughter back together. He wanted you to leave with the idea that he had cut his kid in half. He always closed his show by posing one final question to the audience. He'd say, "I want you to know I wouldn't kill a girl every show, especially my daughter. The real question isn't 'Is it a trick?' but, 'Was it done well?'"

Whoa.

My parents and I never talked about the experience—never. It was powerful, mind-blowing, and completely unforgettable.

Richiardi's approach was a lot like Houdini's in that his act was never about props or the tricks. There were no scenic elements. He used a single black curtain as his backdrop. His style was very minimalist—no flash or flare. His execution was superb—just pure talent. His illusions didn't matter as much as how he presented them—at least not to me. He took the simplest of objects, like a broomstick or a chair, and created miracles with them. He was obviously working without a very big budget, but it didn't deter the audience from enjoying a full experience.

I closely studied his techniques, especially his minimalist style. I'd watch videotapes of his show, which allowed me to rewind and look at each and every frame. I often paused the tape so I could take Polaroid pictures of the frozen images on my television to analyze each step or move at leisure. I wanted to soak up his knowledge and expertise to improve my show.

Talent like Richiardi's is innate. You can't teach that kind of charisma; either you have it, or you don't. If you are lucky enough to be born with it, you can develop your presence. But some people are just not made up that way; it's not in their chemistry. As hard as they try, they will never evolve into an engaging performer. They become duplicators, not innovators. They mimic someone else's talent; they don't create their own art.

As I began to explore other personal influences, I found myself drawn to eccentric personalities like surreal artist Salvador Dalí and one of the greatest filmmakers of all time, Federico Fellini. Dalí was addicted to fame and money. His parents named him Salvador, which means "the savior," because they believed he would be the savior of painting, which was considered to be in great danger at the time from other forms of art. Dalí was often described as a provocateur. He loved creating works that shocked and startled people. He innately understood that, as an artist, garnering any type of reaction from his audience was the best way to seduce them and win their favor. His greatest joy in life was being Salvador Dalí. I can relate to that.

Like Dalí, I am a man with insatiable curiosity. When I have an idea, I turn it into magic. Dalí put all of his discoveries and inventions into his artwork. He used his everyday knowledge and psychological savvy to turn himself into a star. He loved talking about ways to become a genius. His explanation was a simple one. "If you act like a genius, you will be one."

As a child Dalí dreamed of becoming a cook (I worked in my dad's restaurant as a kid). By age seven he wanted to be Napoleon (not a complex I've ever had). Since then, he wanted nothing more than to be Salvador Dalí (all I ever wanted to be was Criss Angel … most of the time). He was an egomaniac who discovered his passion as a young boy, painting his first picture before the age of ten. One of his most famous paintings is *The Persistence of Memory (Soft Watches)*, which was derived from a dream of runny Camembert cheese. It represents a metaphysical image of time devouring itself and everything else, too. There are days I understand that painting better than anyone. It seems like I never have enough time in my life. Much of my art direction and design focuses on Dalí-inspired images. His ability to put an unusual twist on the everyday triggered something in my approach to presenting the same concepts to my audience.

Another important influence on my work is filmmaker Federico Fellini. He had a unique approach when it came to making movies: He viewed cinema not as being about delivering messages so much as it was about raising questions. I just love that concept. It resonated deep within me, reminding me of Richiardi's question at the end of each show. Fellini was six years old when he attended his first circus. He walked into the big top and felt more at home in a circus tent than he did anywhere else. The surroundings had a tremendous impact on him and would greatly influence his filmmaking style. As a child, Fellini staged elaborate puppet shows with his brother, spending hours designing the costumes and the spectacular sets. The process of creating and choreographing the shows was far more intriguing than the content of the play, which made for some very confusing puppet shows.

Years later, Fellini was often questioned by critics who complained they couldn't understand the plots of his films. But he didn't care about critical acclaim. Fellini made films for the art, for the experience he felt. He never thought about his films in terms of dialogue or plot twists, but rather put the emphasis on the images. He would have been a very good silent moviemaker. His lack of interest in dialogue got me thinking about communicating without using words. Ultimately, that's exactly what I did in my off-Broadway show, *MINDFREAK*. I never spoke a word. Fellini believed that when a particular scene has been properly structured and dramatically works, words no longer have any importance. Vitality was everything in a Fellini film. He enjoyed the process of filmmaking in the moment, much more than he did the final image projected on the screen.

There was no guidebook I could read growing up that could possibly have taught me everything I needed to know to achieve my dreams. I researched everyone in whom I found the slightest bit of inspiration. I analyzed how they became successful and figured out how to take their secrets and apply them to my own career. I loved watching shows like

ME AND MY FAT
BOY, MY FIRST
HARLEY.

Behind the Music, which detailed the rise and lives of famous musicians and singers and their journey from teenager to superstar. Madonna is a tremendous example of someone who went to New York with a couple of dollars in her pocket and an enormous dream to conquer the world. She did whatever she had to do until she hit the big time. I admired her commitment and determination. She clearly understood what her market wanted in a performer. She's a great example of someone who developed a unique style, look, and brand, and then marketed herself as a total package, filling a void that everyone else bought in to and tried to copy. She's an innovative genius.

"CRISS HAS INSPIRED a whole generation of magicians. The basic story of any **magician** is more or less the same. When we start out, we see *someone we admired* and wanted to emulate. **The future of magic is very healthy** because we have so much diversity right now. For many years, magic had only one image, and **now that has changed**."

Lance Burton, magician

I wanted to be the person to fill the gaping hole in the world of magic. I was willing to sacrifice and commit myself. You've got to love what you do to have the type of drive and passion to go through the rigors of ascertaining whatever it is you're striving for. You have to know, trust, and like yourself, inside and out. If you want people to believe in what you do, you have to believe in yourself. You must be willing to take risks and do things that might be unconventional to set yourself apart. If you want attention, go out there and grab it. That's what I did. I intentionally chose to present myself in a completely different light as a way of standing apart from other magicians and the conformity of magic. It's been easy to fool people by my appearance. It's part of the illusion. Choosing not to wear a tuxedo and ruffled shirt doesn't make me an evil magician. It surely doesn't make me God or the Devil. Don't be put off by my appearance. Embrace that I'm different. Open your mind to an art form that can transform the impossible right before your eyes. I'm an artist—an artist who is trained to make you believe whatever I choose for you to believe. That doesn't make it real. It makes it magic.

"The **human catalysts for dreamers** are the teachers and encouragers that 'dreamers' encounter throughout their lives. They are *invaluable* in the quest to TURN IDEAS INTO REALITY."

Kevin Carroll
(read this on the side of a Starbucks coffee cup)

By now you know that as a kid, music had a much greater influence on me than magic. As I began developing magic showcases I knew I could draw from my own experiences as someone who not only loves listening to music, but also enjoys the creative process of composing music. I was sure I could couple those interests with my awe-inspiring demonstrations and reach deep into my audiences' hearts and souls.

"**Criss's inventiveness** not only *transcends* the boundaries of traditional magic, but equally **pushes limits** in the musical realm."

Klayton
(Celldweller)

I wanted to discover a way to bring all my talents to the stage and combine them with the influences of my mentors, predecessors, and

MY FIRST APPEARANCE ON HOWARD STERN, WHO HAS BEEN
VERY KIND TO ME.

other artists who greatly influenced my views and the presentation of
my art. I was in a continuous search for that elusive secret that makes
a performer appear evolved, developed, and different. It took years of
rejection, failure, and experimentation to develop into the performer I
am today. I think back to all of the people who said "no" along the way
and wonder what it was they were rejecting.

My image? My art? My performance?

So many critics just didn't get me. I was different from anyone
they'd ever seen. People are uncomfortable with the unfamiliar and
extreme images. I was told numerous times they didn't like the gothic

image and they didn't think I was talented enough. Some even said I was too gross to be entertaining. I used to get so upset by the rejection. I'd literally lie in my bed and cry for hours because some record executive promised he'd call me and never did. And if he did call, he was feeding me basic bullshit about how he was going to sign me but never followed through. I used to put myself through hours of agony waiting and waiting and waiting. It was horrible. It took me years to understand and accept that when something doesn't happen as you'd like it to, it usually means there is a better scenario in the future.

I kept all of the rejection letters I received over the years as my personal inspiration to prove to those doubters they were wrong. For years, their dismissive words brewed in my mind. They haunted me in my sleep. They swirled about until I realized I could actually use the rejection to create a better show. Ultimately, I realized the negative responses actually had a positive influence. Rejection helps you narrow down and focus on the areas of your life that move you, that propel you toward the right path. All of those people who rejected me, sent me away, or said no to me built my drive and strengthened my determination to succeed. I never let them beat me down.

"Christopher has FAILED MORE TIMES than he has succeeded. He was **promised** so many things and **rejected** so many times it's hard to comprehend how *he kept plowing through*. Every time, he picked himself up, dusted himself off, and **just kept on going**. He had this tunnel vision. At the end of THIS TUNNEL WAS HIS DREAM."

J. D., my brother

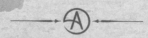

I never wanted to be the "next" anyone. I always wanted to be the first and only Criss Angel. People aren't interested in seeing my version of someone else's trick. The public is smarter and more sophisticated than that. They want originality, creativity, art, and a performance they can't get anywhere else. I am a performer first, above and beyond my skill as a magician, musician, or artist. I understand how to put something together to connect with an audience on an emotional level. Music was an extremely effective way to draw audiences into my fantasy world because it evokes great emotions in people, especially original powerful compositions. Before I began focusing on magic as my art form, I thought it was my destiny to become a drummer in a rock band. I thought being a musician was a lot sexier than being a

AT OZZFEST SIGNING, SIGNING, AND SIGNING FOR THE INCREDIBLE LOYAL AND INDISPENSABLE MEN AND WOMEN OF THE ARMED FORCES.

geeky magician. I never thought magicians were the types of guys who had groupies or a large following. Yeah … they're called the Loyal.

"He has a vision of what he wants and he doesn't let anyone deter him from what he is doing to achieve his goal. Everything that he has been doing is just a testament of his pursuit of his dream. I'm truly amazed by his determination."

Peter Thea,
senior vice president, The Zomba Label Group

LAYING DOWN VOCAL
TRACKS AT THE HIT
FACTORY IN NEW
YORK CITY. MANY,
MANY YEARS AGO.

WITH MY GOOD FRIENDS VINCE NEIL, SULLY ERNA, NINO BETTEN-
COURT, AND SHANNON LARKIN AFTER THE *MF2* MUSIC VIDEO SHOOT.

ROB ZOMBIE AND I ON THE SET OF HIS MOVIE *Devil's Rejects*
JUST BEFORE HE HOSTED MY *Buried Alive* SPECIAL.

I figured out pretty early on that music would not be my best shot at making it. I had to be totally honest with myself if I was going to evolve and develop as a performer and artist. Besides, I was too big a ham to be stuck behind a drum kit for the rest of my life. I had to get out in front, so I put all of my time, attention, and focus on committing to the art of magic. I always understood that music was a fucked industry. I've heard nightmare stories from friends who have record deals about not getting paid earned royalties by record companies that were ripping them off. If I had become a musician, I'm certain you would never have heard my name. I would be on some one-hit-wonder or 1990s flashback show with a host asking, "Where is he now?" For sure my reputation would have been tarnished beyond repair. I think the only career more difficult to be successful in than music must be politics—though I'll never know. Looking back, I am so glad I didn't get a record contract when I was younger. I would have been a flash in the pan. I would've had my fifteen minutes of fame, and then—well, I'm not sure. There was never really another option. Magic was my calling.

Deep down, I understand my strengths and weaknesses. If you're willing to confront your truth, you will be faced with making some hard choices. There's a cause and effect to everything. If you eat hamburgers five times a day, you're going to gain weight. If you hit the gym five days a week, you'll get lean and buff. Life is about choices that make sense for you. I once heard Prince say something like "Life is death without change." I love that statement because it speaks to the assembly-line mentality so many people have in just getting through another day. I've never put restrictions on my imagination. If you can dream it, you can achieve it. I am the kind of person who sees things more in focus and in tune with the choices I make, because I'm always in relentless pursuit of the bigger picture—of living my dream. There are lots of people in this world who live more in the moment, and that's okay, as long as you don't lose sight of your priorities and goals. We have grown so accustomed to living in an instant gratification world, where we expect instant answers and results. If you've ever stayed up late at night watching TV, you'll see a barrage of infomercials promising to deliver immediate results. It doesn't work that way. Trust me—it's a setup for failure. It takes a lot of diligence, persever-

PERFORMING AT A MYSPACE.COM EVENT.

ance, and a tremendous sense of knowing yourself to take the path of most resistance.

Over the years, I've taken bits and pieces from my greatest influences, including parts of Houdini, Richiardi, Dalí, and Fellini, and many more artists and innovators. Evidence of their particular styles can be clearly seen in my work. While my personal approach has emerged into something people perceive as crossing over into areas often associated with dark, satanic cults, gothic, black magic, voodoo, and all sorts of other evil-sounding names, the truth is, it's just a stage persona and it's just me. It's deliberate, and it has worked well in raising the consciousness and curiosity of my loyal fans and people who might be witnessing my art for the first time.

Writing my own music has been a great emotional outlet for me. I always try to tell a story through my art, and music is no exception. I've written songs about relationships and loss and all sorts of life experiences. Writing lyrics is different from creating the visual elements for my shows, though both are definitely reflective of my life. Music is very direct. People can relate to lyrics and subjectively apply the words and meanings to their own lives. If something happens to me that I feel is cool enough to share, I may create a song to bring that to life, or I might incorporate it into my show through a character or a particular demonstration.

A true *MINDFREAK* experience comes from a great audiovisual connection. When both elements come together, the encounter is seamless. Music is imperative to completing my vision and giving people a total audiovisual entertainment event they've come to expect when seeing my show. Without it, the audience notices everything I want them to ignore.

When there's great music that's done well and feels right, you will get lost in all of the auditory sensory stimulation … which is exactly what I want you to do.

The whole culture of music, from the fans to the driven passionate commitment it takes to be a great performer, helped me create a persona that gives people the perception I am more musician than magician. I love it. I prefer it that way. It's much cooler. Because of my image, I can go onstage during a Rob Zombie, Korn, Ice Cube, Godsmack, or Linkin Park concert and not get booed off the stage. I like that I connect with the same fan base as these bands. I'd be lying if I didn't admit to you that I sometimes worry about being accepted in those kinds of settings. I'm not out there with my band—I'm out there pulling a string out of my eye or cutting a quarter out of my forearm. I'm happy to say that I have my fifth album coming out, which means music has turned out to be as big in my life as magic. My record company has a distribution deal with Koch Records, which allows me to work with some incredible best-selling artists. All those years I chased a record deal ... the minute I didn't care about it anymore, record executives came knocking on my door. I guess having the number one show on cable and achieving success is infectious to all of the naysayers.

CHAPTER SEVEN

MINDFREAK

ONE OF MY FIRST S.I.R. STUDIOS SHOWCASES IN
NEW YORK CITY WITH MY BROTHER COSTA.

MINDFREAK: 1. A MODERN-DAY MYSTIFIER WHO USES SKILLS BEYOND THE CATEGORY OF MAGIC. 2. THE RESULT OF SOMETHING INCOMPREHENSIBLE. 3. CRISS ANGEL.

For centuries magic has mostly been seen through "abracadabra," "hocus pocus" eyes. My art is the antithesis of traditional magic. A lot of today's magic is mostly presented as puzzles and tricks. The presentations are lacking originality and a fresh approach to old, tired magic. As for someone like me, I wanted to catapult the art form into the future. The perception of magic is that it's a cheap novelty. If I was going to achieve success, I had to raise the level of expectation in what magic could be every time I performed.

I always hated being referred to as a magician. What I do is so much more than that word generally symbolizes to people. Houdini was labeled a magician even though he was probably more famous for being an escape artist. When I began performing, I wanted to come up with a term that would become synonymous with my image. I wanted to be the only person people thought of when they heard it. I never understood why we live in a world of labels, but it's really hard to avoid being labeled as something, especially when you're different in every imaginable way. Like it or not, most of us are identified by our occupation: doctor, lawyer, teacher, salesman, actor, musician—each is easy to understand in one simple word. You get what I'm talking about. But what if your job were so complex, there were no words in any language to define it? You'd do what I did. You'd make one up.

At first I was labeled as an "illusionist," a term I didn't mind, but to me it's a bit old-school—which I am not. While I generally liked the term "mystifier," it still felt generic. It gave the impression that I use various methods to create a certain effect, but it wasn't provocative enough. I shifted from "mystifier" to "provocateur" for about five minutes. I tried being a "performance artist," but that didn't capture the magic elements at all. Labels suck.

I came up with the word "MINDFREAK" because I wanted a term that I thought was cool and about which people didn't have any preconceived notions. I didn't want to be pigeonholed professionally by a title that my peers already personified.

So, where did "MINDFREAK" come from? It started with me doodling a million thoughts on a piece of paper. The term doesn't limit me to one particular area. I knew my performances were considered to be a little freaky. I intentionally design my demonstrations to manipulate people's minds—play with their heads. Some people even believe I'm a spooky guy with supernatural powers, which makes me some sort of freak of nature. I began playing with all of these words, twisting them around, tying them together, and breaking them apart until I had an epiphany.

To be honest, the best word I could think of to describe what I do was *mind-fuck*. It really sums up the Criss Angel experience. If I could have gotten away with it, I would have used it, but I knew the marketability of the term would be very limited. Also, my good friends Penn and Teller had already branded their Showtime series *Bullshit!* Using another curse word for my show's title reeked a little of duplicating the image they were going for. I didn't want people to think I was ripping them off, especially because what I do onstage is really different from their style. Besides, I think most people get what I mean by *MINDFREAK*. Also, I wanted to create a word that would invent a new meaning in the English language. I've actually heard people use

"MINDFREAK" in everyday conversation. That's a really cool feeling. The only thing that could top that is to someday see the word *MINDFREAK* in the dictionary. In retrospect it has definitely worked better than going for the obvious. It allows me the creative freedom to change it up a bit and not be tied to any particular area in my performances. I like having that option.

When it comes to developing demonstrations, I mostly think about what interests me, what pleases me, and what I would like to see onstage. That's how I embark on every journey that evolves into a MINDFREAK. My ideas come both from everyday experiences and my innermost fantasies. Sometimes I get an idea driving in my car or sitting on an airplane, where there's total separation from the phone and e-mail. Sometimes I get ideas in the shower, because no one can bother me there and I'm very relaxed. I've even been known to get inspired while lying in bed, moments before I fall asleep. I was once on vacation in the Caribbean when I noticed there were ceiling fans all around. I studied the one over my head as it spun round and round. As I lay there, I began to think about different ways of doing a demonstration that involved my reading someone's mind and then making a spinning fan spontaneously stop so their thought could appear in ashes on the top side of the fan paddle.

Impossible, right? Wrong. I actually figured out a way to make that one work.

I think of these types of improbable tasks because I have the wonderment of a child. That freedom of thought allows me to conjure up the impossible and make it possible. A child looks at things in a very innocent way. There are no restrictions, no rules, and no law of gravity. When exactly do most of us lose that freedom? Kids can turn a tape recorder into a flying saucer because their imaginations are limitless. Children are clean slates who haven't yet been told by society that a tape recorder can't be a flying saucer, so they can sit for hours and act out all sorts of scenes in their heads about space and spaceships, Martians, Lilliputians, and space monsters if they want to.   .

"One of **my greatest satisfactions** is to share with Criss THE THRILL he has after he accomplishes something that was a figment of his imagination and that HE MADE COME TRUE. He made it real and tangible. He's like a child who sees something for the first time. *It's magical—it's real magic.*"

Costa, my brother

ONE OF THE FIRST PICTURES OF ME WITH SIEGFRIED AND ROY, AFTER THEY PERFORMED AT THE MIRAGE IN LAS VEGAS.

As an adult, I have allowed myself the same freedom of thought I had as a child. I never put rules or boundaries on what is possible. I have no preconceived notion about what is acceptable or unacceptable behavior when it comes to performing and creating. Nothing is off-limits. In fact, there are no limits. In my imaginary surrealistic world, there is no impossibility.

Unlike many areas of the entertainment business, being a magician is not as fickle as, say, the life of an actor, singer, or a band. Eventually they all come and go. Styles change. Tastes change. Magic is a rare form of entertainment that has remained incredibly stable. People like Penn and Teller, Lance Burton, and Siegfried and Roy have had long, successful careers, though Roy's tragic accident is a reminder that what we all do is very dangerous and very real.

"**Criss Angel** is *the heir apparent to Harry Houdini* and is responsible for **magic's resurgence** today."

Johnny Thompson,
The Great Thomsoni/Magician

There are so few leaders in magic. Most magicians working today are followers. They're doing the same tricks that have been done for decades. It's all very cookie-cutter. The energy of the performer dictates the energy of the show. This is true for all great performers past and present, whether it's performers like Elvis Presley or Prince or film stars like Angelina Jolie or Johnny Depp. The magnitude of their charisma has always been a surefire barometer of the success of their acts. Most magicians performing today lack that charisma and have not spent the necessary time to develop it. They've become so caught up in the tricks and technical aspects that go into making up their show that they've forgotten about selling the audience the most important thing—themselves. As a performer, I can never forget my fans, the Loyal. They're the reason I do what I do.

Magic is a business of longevity, but given the number of magicians in the world, it's also an art that hasn't produced a lot of superstars over the years, especially compared to other areas in the world of entertainment. Think about this: How many magicians can you name off the top of your head?

I recently attended a magic convention and was both amazed and a little dismayed that most of the show was the same crap I saw when I was a kid attending these same kinds of conventions. It seems like magic has gotten stuck in a time warp. There's a huge public demand for magic. Granted, it is much more of a niche thing than music or films, but there are so few people practicing magic at a higher level. Magic is embedded in all forms of entertainment. For example, when you go to the movies, there's usually some kind of a special effect that defies reality. There's a certain feeling you get when you are swept up by the fantasy on the screen. Do you ever look at the screen and wonder how they are doing that? Usually, the answer is no. You just allow the movie to be what it is while you enjoy and connect to the story.

"*Magic has traditionally* had throughout the years more of a **family audience**, where you have kids and adults and senior citizens, but you tend to lose the audience there when they get to be TEENAGERS OR IN THEIR TWENTIES. Criss, because of the

GOTTA DO WHAT YOU GOTTA DO TO GET THE BAD BOYS OF MAGIC, PENN AND TELLER, TO COME ON MY SHOW.

way he PRESENTS MAGIC and *his sensibility*, has been able to tap into this market."

Lance Burton, magician

There are more magicians living in Las Vegas than there are anywhere else in the world. Why? Because two hundred fifty thousand tourists every three days want to be entertained. Magic is a form of entertainment that consistently draws crowds. It's a proven entity. Even a lousy magician doing cheesy, hokey, old-school crap can make a great living. The general public doesn't know there's so much more available to them than a tuxedo-clad guy pulling rabbits out of hats and sawing a leotard-wearing woman in half. Someone like Lance Burton, a good friend and a great magician, does a very traditional show, but he does it better than anyone else in the world today. Penn and Teller, also good friends, have incorporated comedy and clever magic into their show, giving it a more sophisticated, artsy feel than a traditional magic act. The Amazing Jonathan, another compatriot of mine, has developed a very funny show, but he's not really doing a lot of magic so much as he is doing comedy.

There are countless wannabes. I never wanted to be anyone but Criss Angel. The public expects a magic show to be like something they've seen before. The art of magic is precious. Magicians have never really garnered the kind of respect that actors or musicians get. I think it's because there are so many categories that magicians fall into, such as the large-scale illusionist and the parlor magician. Close-up magic allows the audience to follow along while the magician uses coins, cards, or anything small you can pull out of your pocket or borrow from them. These performers are very good at using their hands as tools to manipulate our minds. You will always be entertained by their type of magic. To me, it's like listening to someone play the piano. I'm always astonishingly entertained by that. A good close-up magician usually plays to a small audience. How do you make a huge impact when you perform for half a dozen people at a time? How can you achieve the same level of success as a large-scale illusionist when you spend all of your time selling the prop over the magician?

It's so important to develop a personality that people will identify with your magic. You never want your audience to get bored with you. It's your goal to understand what people are going to respond to. People's first impressions are not necessarily based on what they see. They're based on years of programming to believe that what they see is good, bad, positive, negative, mean, nice—whatever their perception is of your appearance. I've spent my entire professional life being judged by my look. Some people say I'm too dark, too gothic, too rap, too rock. Why is that image negative to some people and cool to others? Years of certain images' being ingrained into people's minds and what those images conjure up. For example, have you ever walked down the street and seen someone who caused you to worry for your safety? Maybe you took a wide step away or held your purse a little tighter? In your mind, you've been programmed to believe how you should judge a person. We all do it. Maybe it's the clothes someone wears or the way they do their hair and makeup. Perhaps you judge someone if they're overweight, have a bad complexion, or are unkempt? If you were blind, you'd be forced to judge people for who they are on the inside. You'd discover their hearts and connect to the way they speak as opposed to how they look. I don't care how anyone looks—I try to treat people equally because that is how I want to be treated. Believe me, it hasn't always been easy!

Magic is taking the impossible and saying, "Hey, look at this situation." It has to come from one's soul. The art has to live and breathe and be synonymous with the person performing. You can take a mediocre performer, put him in the most amazing Cirque du Soleil show, and he'll still be mediocre, because it's just not in his soul. He's lacking passion. When people try to re-create my demonstrations, they don't know what my intention was when I created it. They approach it from a superficial perspective without knowing my motivation. They might be able to re-create or emulate the physicality of what I am doing, but they will never be able to demonstrate the spirituality, the meaning, or the heart of where that stuff comes from. They can rip me off, but they can't steal my soul. That's the difference between making a connection and just going through the motions.

There's real danger in most everything I attempt. I don't want to die, but risk is a part of what I do. I could die crossing the street. You never know what's going to happen. I know for sure you can't live your life in fear. I don't. I embrace the danger that's involved in my day-to-day life. It makes me cautious. I don't identify myself as a stuntman, even though so much of what I do involves stunts at the highest level. I love pushing the envelope—my own envelope. I'm willing to take chances and have been successful in utilizing my ability and my art. I'm like a high jumper who visualizes what the jump looks like so he can get over the bar, or a ball player who has to "be the ball."

I operate as a general practitioner because I can do in excess of two hundred effects during a season of shooting *MINDFREAK*. Some people will spend a lifetime learning and perfecting coin magic or card

THIS STUNT SENT ME TO THE HOSPITAL WHERE SURGERY WAS PERFORMED ON MY LEG. THIS PICTURE DEPICTS THE ACTUAL MOMENT WHEN I WAS BURNED. GOOD THING THE OUTFIT DIDN'T SURVIVE.

WITH MY MOM IN THE HOSPITAL AFTER THE ACCIDENT.

tricks. I play around in those areas, but I never mastered any one specific thing. There are lots of people working who are far more skilled at using a deck of cards or coins than I am, but I guarantee you'll fall asleep watching them, because they don't understand how to make a connection with their audience and the relevance of engaging them on an emotional level. My wide range of skills has been a benefit in my career. My diversity allows me to be freer when creating new and extremely challenging demonstrations. One day I may be doing something using a wine bottle, a gum ball, or a card trick, and the next I am hypnotizing or levitating someone, making an elephant disappear, or doing a motorcycle jump with an illusion twist. If a demonstration doesn't work the way I want it to, I have to figure out another way to do it—and sometimes in the middle of the failing demonstration. I can't let millions of television viewers see me screw up. I have mastered using my personality to cover up failing effects.

So much of what I do has never been done before, and when it comes to life-or-death demonstrations, there's no cutting corners. It is essential to take the proper time to study the mock-up model, play around with it, create different scenarios, and figure out how it will work and what could possibly go wrong. I never know what to expect, but for every challenge, I am determined to find a solution so I can bring that seedling of an idea to life. Often, my solutions have a domino effect, creating other problems that need to be rectified as well so that it all comes together as an entire unit.

Once a life-size model of my concept has been created, I perform what I call a "garbage bag" test. It's a quick, inexpensive trial run that gives my team and me the opportunity to experience the demonstration on a smaller scale to avoid problems and setbacks during the actual stunt. Something on paper can look like it will work, but you never

THE FIRST FIRE TEST FOR *Supernatural* AND I HAVE THE SCARS TO PROVE IT.

know until you've put it to a technical test. The garbage bag test gives us the chance to look at everything that could go wrong and is especially important when my life is in real danger. You have to take every potential pitfall into account to assure success. Without this process, I would have killed myself a long time ago.

Rest assured: I do my homework before attempting anything crazy so I can be as safe as possible. These days, unfortunately, I just don't have the luxury of practicing, because the pace of my television series is frenetic and time-sensitive. We're shooting eighteen to twenty-hour workdays for the show, and although I know conceptually that everything I do will work, sometimes I have to walk out there and hope it all comes together. It's a blessing and a curse. It's a blessing because I am getting really good at improvisational performance, and it's a curse because I would rather have the opportunity to develop the material further and thoroughly work it out before anyone sees it. Somehow, we still always manage to pull off the presentation seamlessly within the budgetary constraints and technical parameters. That's showbiz!

Thankfully, I have assembled an excellent team of people who help me prepare on every level for the demonstrations I perform. John Farrell, my production designer, is one of my first stops. He's been working with me for thirteen years. A scenic and direction designer, his job is to coordinate all of the illusions and the magic team. He does everything from creating sets to figuring out wardrobe with my stylist. He does a little bit of everything. John is excellent at taking my concepts and creations, turning them into mechanical drawings, and looking at the idea in a practical way to see if it can work. Over the years, I've given John an education in illusions, how they technically function, and the creative essential elements of theatrical design for a live show, and he helps me bring my stick-figure ideas to life in the biggest way. He is the man who can take my vision and help me visually bring it to life.

RIGHT
A moment
from the
MINDFREAK
video shoot.

BELOW
My alternate ego
"Crissy" and her
newborn babies.

TOP My OCC season one *MINDFREAK* chopper.

BOTTOM A moment from the second season's desert sequence, which has a spirit that will resonate in my future live show.

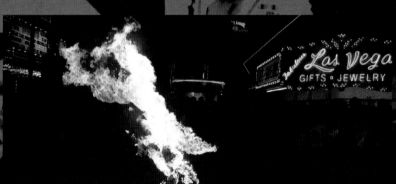

TOP Inspired by Dalí.

BOTTOM Burned alive on Fremont Street
during the first season of *MINDFREAK*.

BOTTOM This picture was taken just after
I went 185 mph on my bike.

ABOVE Erich growing the surreal family.

BELOW Floating in the desert in a surreal vignette.

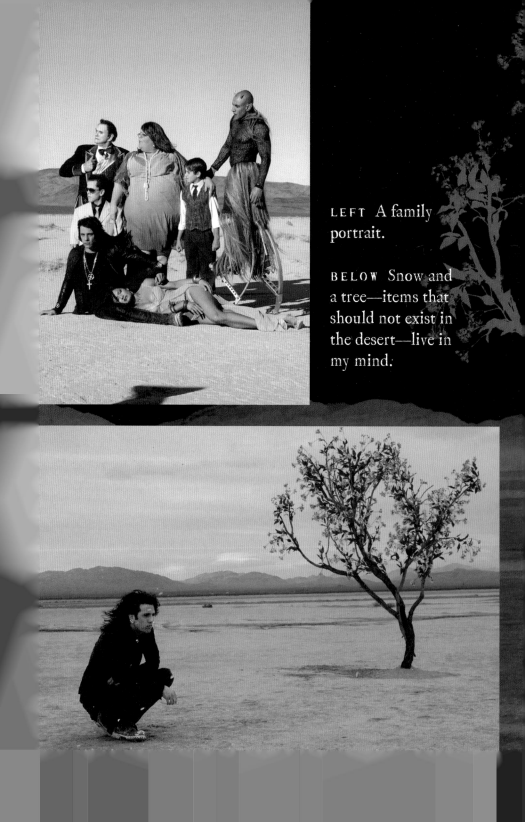

LEFT A family portrait.

BELOW Snow and a tree—items that should not exist in the desert—live in my mind.

TOP Getting shut out once again.

BELOW Time doesn't stand still for anyone.

TOP My Kount's Custom MF2 chopper for
the second season of *MINDFREAK*.

BELOW One of my signature poses
that I first did in the early 1990s.

"I MET CRISS IN NEW YORK in 1992. I was working on the Broadway show production of *Grease*. The owner of the company I was working for told me about a young up-and-coming magician he knew. Herb had known Criss for a few years. *He described his magic to me as being a little obscure. What an understatement!* He told me Criss was looking for someone to do some sketches and drawings for him to help ILLUSTRATE HIS CONCEPTS and ideas. In those days, I took every job I could get my hands on. Criss called me the next day and **immediately began pitching his idea** for a live show that mixed rock and roll with magic. When we got together, Criss showed me his drawings. I was blown away. I HAD NEVER SEEN ANYTHING LIKE IT BEFORE. He literally had no money to pay me, but *I believed in what I saw*. When it came to magic, Criss's way of thinking was different from anyone I had ever met. What started out as a six-week gig has turned into a thirteen-year relationship."

John Farrell, my production designer

I met Michael Blum at a production meeting after I had made a deal with A&E to do *MINDFREAK*. A&E wanted me to use network-approved show runners (producers with experience whom the network

121

knows and trusts to deliver finished shows on time and on budget). At the time, Michael was working for a production company that was running several shows. As we progressed, I recognized Michael was really focused on running *MINDFREAK*. So I hired him to be one of my executive producers, which allowed us to put together a team of people to create more magic and produce far more interesting shows. Once we have the mechanicals done, we take the concept to a fabricator who is right for that particular idea. Since I've been doing this for so long, I have a great set of contacts and know exactly who to go to for any particular type of setup. I've worked with Hollywood special-effects legends as well as pyrotechnic experts, illusion fabricators, costume and wardrobe consultants, and lighting designers. I never want to be the smartest guy in the room. Someone always knows more or has more experience. I am a smart enough guy to know the value in tapping into those incredible brain trusts. My network is wide and bizarre, and it is an integral part of creating unforgettable demonstrations.

"In **the history of U.S. television**, there has never been another maGICIan who has as many hours of magic-driven primetime programming as **Criss Angel** and *MINDFREAK*."

Dave Baram, my manager

The fact that we can produce a weekly series that entails so many different technical elements is in itself a tremendous feat and nothing short of magic. The logistics for producing a show like *MINDFREAK* are greater than almost any other type of series on the air. The sheer volume of material that we go through—more than two hundred demonstrations and effects per season—is insane. Some magicians wouldn't create this number of effects in a lifetime. We are held up to a standard that no other television show has to deal with. Audiences are immune to the spectacular things they see. They've seen so many movies with wild special effects, and are familiar with industrial lighting and movie magic. Nothing fazes them anymore. That means my team and I have to work that much harder to truly do it live and in public places.

After an episode of *MINDFREAK* airs, a zillion amateur magicians go into Internet chat rooms to discuss the show. I don't have time to read those chats, but I'm amused about what I hear. If they don't understand how I do something, the only solution they can find is that it must be trick photography. Let me make this very clear: I never use trick photography—what you see is what you get—though I have been known to trick the camera every now and then. When you surround yourself with the best people who are experts in their given areas, and you listen to their insights and ideas like I do, I can collectively create demonstrations that blow the audience away. Everything you see me do on television I must be able to do live. The magician's code is such that I believe before I can work in front of a camera, I must be able to perform it as a stage act. Just when people think they have me figured out, I have to throw a twist in there, because as a performer, I always strive to give people the unexpected. That's what I call a MINDFREAK.

"Within the magic community, a lot of magicians, especially the amateurs, want to expose various methods to show HOW CLEVER THEY are. Criss Angel has DONE MORE FOR MAGIC

with one of his television episodes than all of the
exposing shows put together."

Banachek, mentalist

If you want to further advance magic, do better magic. I never want
to stop learning. The minute you think you know everything is the kiss
of death. I always want to learn new tricks. Before my television show,
I had more opportunities to get out and just do magic for the love of
the art. It wasn't about making money or being famous. It was because
I love what I do, and I adore the organic responses of wonderment and
appreciation. There's not a better feeling in the world than the sensation I get after I've learned a new move. I always want to be able to
capture the feeling I used to get as a boy practicing magic for hours
and hours until I got it right. The *art* is the reason I got into this business—it's what I go back to every chance I get.

As a performer, I enjoy doing a live show so much more than something that's being shot for television. It's not the cameras so much as
it is the doubt that you, the viewer, have regarding the authenticity of
what you see on TV. When you watch magic on television, you're seeing it from a one-dimensional perspective you would never have during
a live show. I can draw an audience in, captivate their imaginations, and
dazzle them by using them in the effect. The closer I can get, the more
direct contact I make. I can touch. I can come in so close that certain
elements are out of your visual perception. I can't do that on camera,
so I am constantly looking for ways to present the material so the authenticity is not challenged—yet the integrity of the effect is protected.
MINDFREAK is shot in real time. What you see is what you get.

In recent years, magic hadn't really worked well when presented
in that venue. Most tried to present the magic show as if the viewing

THE FIRST TIME I PERFORMED METAMORPHOSIS ON TV WITH THE
CAST OF CREATURES I DESIGNED AND BUILT AT MY FAMILY HOME.
THIS WAS THE END POSE OF THE VIGNETTE.

audience were in a live theater, which was very boring to the TV viewer.
I have tried to find a balance between maintaining the integrity of the
effect and being mindful of what it looks like to the viewing audience at
home. The pace and slickness of contemporary television programming
doesn't use magic to hold your attention. My challenge was to keep my
viewers interested, so I began to ask questions about ways to shoot the
demonstrations and methods of delivering that footage through editing
without digital special effects. The budget doesn't allow me to shoot the
television show like a film. I don't have days to block out shots or cre-

ME AND MINX CATCHING A CATNAP WHILE SHOOTING SEASON ONE
OF *MINDFREAK*.

ate special effects. It's a form of reality television—or surreality television. The upside for me as a performer is that the hectic pace and the quantity of material have made me a much better thinker and a more spontaneous and engaging performer.

A live show is a completely different experience for me as a performer and for you as my audience: I am able to take people to places they would never otherwise experience. The emotional connection is like a passageway to a private world—my private world. Fantasy and the great unknown have always fascinated people. People want to hear what I sound like live, see what I look like, witness how I approach a poetic or a life-threatening moment in front of their eyes. The wonderment, the unexpected, the moment of "wow" is something I live for.

There's a connection and an intimacy that can never really be fully achieved through television. In a live show, I'm on a presidium that's as wide as sixty feet and up to fifty feet deep. It can be anywhere from twenty-seven to thirty feet tall. I know there's going to be a certain number of people in the audience, how many seats the theater has and how it's configured, and I can stage the show to give the audience the best possible experience. I can design the demonstrations to appear intimate yet be larger-than-life.

I'm very different onstage as Criss Angel than I am offstage. Onstage I want people to see me as charismatic, powerful, passionate, larger-than-life, caring, and appreciative. Because of the way I look, some people probably think I have a bad attitude or have more of a rock star mentality. Maybe they think I'm not approachable or even am a little scary and intimidating. I thought the rock-and-roll culture represented who I was better than donning a tuxedo and ruffled shirt. I want to be able to do anything, be anyone I choose. I can create another persona that I want people to accept at any time, so I am always trying different angles of me and how I want people to see me. The reality is, I'm like everybody else. There are many different sides to my personality, with deep emotions and feelings. And when I'm performing and creating, I'm Criss Angel, the larger-than-life, badass MINDFREAK.

Offstage, the word I hear most often when other people describe me is nice. Don't let the rumor get out, okay? The truth is, I'm just a regular guy. I try to stay approachable, grounded, and down-to-earth. The people around me appreciate those traits. Staying that way helps me in all areas of my professional and personal lives.

"I think Criss surprises people when they meet him. When his fans, the loyal, meet him face-to-face, they're always *blown away*. His personality and **warmth** are very awe-inspiring. He is an approachable celebrity. He loves the interaction. He's a pretty normal guy who happens to do some **extraordinary things**. He loves what he does and enjoys being able *to share his gifts* with other people. He comes up with stuff off the cuff all the time. I think he's the best at that."

George, my cousin

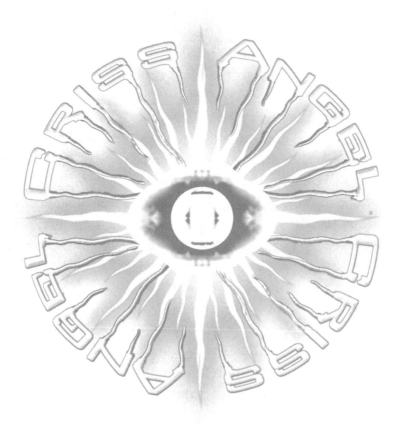

CHAPTER EIGHT

SUCCEEDING

IN FRONT OF THE *MINDFREAK* BROADWAY
MARQUEE, 2001. (P.S. I HATE WHITE LIMOS.)

In September 2001, just after the attacks of

9/11, I went to my mother and told her I needed to mortgage our family home. I wanted to take that money and use it to stage an off-Broadway show in New York City. My family believed in me enough to give me the go-ahead. I didn't care if I had to work five jobs for the next fifty years to pay it back, I would. I took that money and put it where my mouth was.

In my mind, this was the birth of my first *real* show, *MINDFREAK*. It was a huge risk. After the attacks in New York, theater on Broadway was virtually shut down. Tourists weren't coming into the city, and people were definitely not spending money to see a show. Everyone told me I was nuts. Financial experts and Broadway veterans all said it couldn't be done, that I was setting myself up for failure. Worse yet, I was risking my family's home—the last of our money, our security. At a time, in a nation and a city where security was flawed and fractured, I was choosing to take the biggest risk of my life.

I'd had countless disappointments from people in whom I had placed my faith. I realized that was my biggest mistake: believing in people who never delivered. It was a seemingly endless stream of one bullshit artist after another. In the end, I realized I believed in myself more than anyone else would ever believe in me. No one could serve my interests better than I. It was clear that too many people had overpromised and underdelivered, something I try never to do. It was time to take control. If I were going to make it, I'd have to create my own opportunities. I was willing to live by the sword or die by it.

"I've never represented a client nor have I worked with an artist that has **the determination or the drive** that Criss has. He even bet *his mom's house* on it."

Peter Thea,
senior vice president, The Zomba Label Group

It took me twelve years of insane commitment to finally begin breaking through professionally. Throughout the years leading up to that first live show, I had placed much of my fate in other people's hands. These were powerful and connected people who told me they could manage me. They promised the world yet delivered tiny, microscopic pieces of nothing. Empty promises. Words—mere words. No action. I always waited for these people to deliver. They never did. This guy was signing me to a record contract. That guy was setting me up with backers for my Broadway show. Promises of this deal and that deal that never reflected the agreement we made. The truth was always one hundred and eighty degrees different from the offer made face-to-face. These people wanted to own everything I worked so hard to create and build.

What did they mean, *own?*

I've worked my whole life for this.

I created all of this—therefore, *I* own it.

I never entered into a deal where I knew I would end up resenting the other party or parties involved. People offered to be my partner, to work toward building the bigger picture; but in the end, that never happened, either.

I had a pretty good team of people around me at the time, but I had made a lot of changes to get that good team to become a great team. I became a lot stronger as a person because of some of the decisions I had to make. I was the executive producer, and therefore it was my responsibility to run the business aspect of staging the live show in addition to my creative responsibilities—not to mention my role as the star of the show. I wore a lot of hats to make sure I would not fail. I could not fail. Failure was not an option.

Up to this point, so many people had rejected me along the way. I remember telling them they were betting on the wrong horse. I tried to raise the money for the show through private investors, through my agents, through anyone and everyone I met along the way. If they'd just come spend some time to see what I was all about, I knew they'd get it.

Still, everybody told me I was nuts. They warned me not to go through with it. Established Broadway shows were closing. I didn't care. I was determined to get my show up and running. I saw the opening. I envisioned the opportunity. I went for it. I did whatever I had to do to make sure I sold enough tickets to cover my weekly overhead.

Word was out. Criss Angel and *MINDFREAK* were becoming the hottest ticket in town. *MINDFREAK* became a bonafide hit. I turned my initial $360,000 investment into millions of dollars in revenue during my fourteen-month run off-Broadway. Not only was I able to repay the mortgage on our house, I began to build a name and reputation as a leader and innovator in magic. More important to me was the sense of accomplishment I felt in pulling off the show when so many people told me it was impossible.

The success of the live show garnered the attention of many television executives. After several meetings with different networks and

THIS WAS TAKEN DURING THE FIRST PHOTO SESSION FROM MY BROADWAY RUN OF *MINDFREAK* IN 2001.

cable channels, I struck my first television deal with the ABC Family Channel. They contracted to do *MINDFREAK* as a one-hour Halloween special as part of their "Thirteen Nights of Halloween" campaign. It was the number-one-rated show for the thirteen nights of original programming. Because of the success of the TV special, my off-Broadway show began to sell out. I was actually beginning to make some money, and the success of that first special led to my second.

My second Halloween television special, called *Supernatural,* was with the Sci Fi Channel. I busted my ass to deliver the best show I could. Again, because of the lack of budget to do the show I wanted to

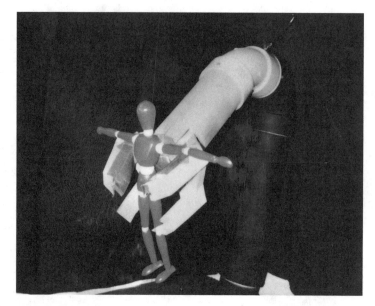

do, I once again found myself donning a lot of different hats to pull it off. I enlisted the help of my brothers and cousins, and together as a family we worked around the clock to give the Sci Fi Channel the best Halloween special we could. Even though they promised to allocate a substantial marketing budget toward the show, they ended up not supporting it at all. They had expected *Scare Tactics*, hosted by Shannen Doherty, to be their big hit. I was the lead-in show.

With no prepublicity or promotion, we kicked ass in the ratings and received great reviews from the media. Because I am a man of principle, I wrote the president of the Sci Fi Channel a letter after the show aired. I was extremely upset about the broken promises and lack of support. I didn't care if my television career would be forever marred by writing the letter—I felt I had nothing to lose. I had built everything I had up to this point by myself and with the complete support of my family. There was nothing the president of the network could do to hurt me.

He's not "the man."

I'm the man.

I create my own destiny, my own luck, my own opportunity.

PERFORMING THE HUMBODIK ON MY SECOND HALLOWEEN
TELEVISION SPECIAL, *Supernatural*.

BURNED ALIVE, FIRST PERFORMED ON *Supernatural*.

No one has control over me—I can always be successful. I wasn't too proud to go back and do kids' parties if I had to.

I didn't care.

I wrote the letter.

I expressed my disappointment and frustration over the huge promises that had been made and not fulfilled. Once again, they bet on the wrong horse. Like my father taught me, that which does not kill you, makes you stronger. I was getting stronger by the day.

I grew up believing that a man is as good as his word. If I tell you I'm going to do something, it gets done. I don't make promises I can't keep. The time and energy spent waiting for something that may or may not ever materialize should have been allocated toward building something. Wasted time. Wasted energy.

As my career began to explode, it became obvious I needed someone who could help guide and support the direction I was headed in. From the moment I met Dave Baram in late 2004, I knew I would be represented and managed by him for the rest of my career. We are blood brothers. We literally cut our hands, let the blood seep through, and shook on our deal. We have no paper contract. We have no need for one. Our commitment is mutual. Our goals are shared.

We both come from blue-collar families in the New York metropolitan area. We understand the influence that has had on our careers. Our work ethic is similar. As an amateur magician himself, Dave gets my need to succeed and my unflinching drive to get there. Every now and then someone comes into your life who you just click with. You get them and they totally understand you from the inside out. Even though we haven't known each other very long, I feel as if he is one of my oldest friends. I trust him with my life. After all of the bullshit professional relationships I've had in the past, I wasn't sure I'd ever give my trust again … but I did.

Dave is president of The Firm, one of the largest talent management companies in Hollywood. He runs a $60 million business, but you'd

DAVE AND I HANGING.

never know it from meeting him. He's the most unassuming man. He attended Harvard Law School and practiced law in Los Angeles for ten years before becoming a partner in The Firm. A manager's job is to be the CEO of his client's career. That could mean hiring a new stylist to soften my image or telling me to go get a haircut and drop the gothic makeup. He is a visionary whose expertise is making his clients better and more successful. With all of the different business interests I have going on, it's nice to have someone like Dave who can manage and handle the various obligations each of those areas demand from me. He's not just my manager, he is also coexecutive producer of the *MINDFREAK* series.

As an artist, my attention and focus are on creating the next demonstration for my television show or getting into the recording studio to cut my next soundtrack. A manager helps an artist build and market his brand, whether it's me as an individual or my permanent live show in Las Vegas.

"I immediately knew **Criss was a star**. There's no question about it in my mind. Criss did something in the magic world I HAD never before WITNESSED. He cultivated a rock star image and developed a loyal fan base the way a rock-and-roll band would do. He didn't need a hit single on the radio or a hit television series for that fan base to care about what he was going to do next. HIS FANS, WHO WE CALL *the Loyal*, ARE VERY DEVOTED. Within forty-eight hours of meeting, Criss proved to me **he was willing to do whatever it would take** to move him to the next level in his career. His **openness and dedication** were refreshingly appealing."

Dave Baram, my manager

Within six months of meeting Dave, I had completely transformed myself. I wanted to go in a different direction with my image. I felt I was getting pigeonholed by the gothic look. Dave was convinced I needed to soften my looks to reach a wider audience, something I would need to do if we were going to be successful in selling *MINDFREAK* as a television show. Dave and I looked at my long-term career plan. We didn't want to do just another television special. The odds were against me, so we wanted to create deeper entertainment, with defined story elements and a sense of dramatic theater—to do a series that would keep viewers coming back every week. When you do new things, networks can be skittish about getting behind a project. We were lucky to get offers from several networks, but A&E were believers from the very beginning.

CHAPTER NINE

DON'T BELIEVE
YOUR EYES

THE FIRST TIME I EVER PUBLICLY WALKED UP THE SIDE OF A
BUILDING DURING MY *Supernatural* TV SPECIAL. TAKE NOTE
OF THE UMBRELLA—INFLUENCED BY CHARLIE CHAPLIN.

I pretty much believe almost nothing of what I hear and half of what I see. Because of my occupation, logical explanations have made me accept that most of what people see as supernatural doesn't exist. Until I see something that cannot be explained or that I can't reproduce, I stand by my conviction that the world is full of lots of hocus pocus bullshit. If I see something that seems unlikely or impossible, I work backward until I figure it out. For years I was consumed with the great urban legend that D. D. Hume had floated from one building to another. It turns out it was nothing more than a myth. However, in my study of how it might have been possible, I spent years developing and devising a way that I could pull off the impossible. How could I float from one building to another located across the street in the middle of the day? No one had ever done this before, but because I have no rules or limitations on what I can do, I figured it out. Can I fly? Float? Levitate? You can be the judge of that.

Magic is an art form with many various subgenres. I perceive myself to be an artist who uses many of those subgenres as tools to connect with my audience, including mentalism, hypnosis, illusion, performance art, stunts, escapes, and so on. Most of these subgenres take elements from many worlds of performance and mix them together to create what could be said to be a distinctly different performance. For example, a magician uses the skills of a conjuror to create the illusion of magical powers. A mentalist mixes the skills of a conjuror with those of a psychologist to create the illusion he is able to read the minds of his audience members. A hypnotist may mix all of the above to give the impression he can somehow control minds at will. Each of these subgenres has its own distinct feeling when performed. However, all of them take influences from one another.

A good magician must understand the way people think. After all, his entire job is to ultimately deceive his audience. By gaining a better understanding of the way people think, the performer is better able to create the strongest impact with his magical effects.

Many people confuse the various subgenres of magic with paranormal or supernatural activity. It's simply not the case. Occurrences that cannot be rationally explained are often the subject of controversy because they do not fit into the established framework of reality. Take phenomena such as UFO sightings. They cannot be fully explained or accurately reproduced, so mainstream science must attribute them to something to justify their existence as asteroid activity or universal holes. If it cannot be reproduced, it cannot be explained. In magic, everything can be reproduced and therefore it can be explained, making "super" powers the only *inexplicable* impossibility.

Salvador Dalí for example, explored visions resulting from various altered states of mind in his work, such as his famous melting-clock image discussed in Chapter Six. Hallucinations stem from the brain's interpreting very unusual phenomena as common and familiar. The brain reads a mirage as water because it looks so incredibly similar. Therein lies the trick.

Paranormal

Seemingly outside normal sensory channels; extrasensory. *Not in* accordance *with* scientific laws.

"The *most beautiful thing* we can experience **is the mysterious**. It is the source of all true art and all science. He to whom *this emotion* is a stranger, who can no longer pause TO WONDER AND STAND RAPT IN AWE, is as good as dead: his eyes are closed."

Albert Einstein

A lot of people have made big money by presenting themselves as having some type of paranormal gift. This phenomenon exists because of the most basic human need to want to believe. At its core, faith is the belief in something you cannot see but know, without a doubt, exists. I can get behind faith from a religious standpoint, but I cannot support the charlatans who go around masquerading as psychic, clairvoyant, parapsychological, psychokinetic, supernormal, supranormal, telegnostic, telepathic, channelers, mediums, communicators to the "other side," and every other type of supposed paranormal or supernatural being who preys on human weakness and vulnerability for personal gain. If these people truly existed, why didn't they predict the catastrophes of Hurricane Katrina, 9/11, or the Holocaust?

IN MY TABLEAU POSE AS I WALKED ON WATER AT THE
ALADDIN POOL.

As a species, we are curious by nature. It's no wonder so many people are constantly in search of signs, answers, and information from dead relatives and loved ones. They want to believe it's possible to speak with the dead—if for no other reason than it gives comfort or eases a hardship. If it were possible, I'd talk to my father every day. Sadly, it is not. Believing in psychics and mediums is a lot easier than working for answers that come with comfort and peace. As I stated earlier, until I personally see something that can't be explained or reproduced, I am very skeptical that paranormal or supernatural activity exists.

There are lots of people who have dedicated their lives to prove or disprove the existence of paranormal claims. James "the Amazing" Randi is one of the best known investigators of psychic, supernatural, and magical claims dealing with subjects that border on both science and mythology. Assaulting claims that a paranormal world exists is his life's work. He has exposed many would-be psychics, healers, mediums, and even a few television evangelists along the way. Randi is so convinced of his position on paranormal activity, he has offered a $1 million prize to anyone who can show, under proper observation conditions, evidence of any paranormal, supernatural, or occult power or event. In forty years, after numerous attempts and failures, no one has successfully claimed the prize. Why would anyone who possessed such skill, such power, such a gift, be working for $45 an hour when they could claim the million dollars? It's simple. They're frauds.

SUPERNATURAL

1 : OF OR RELATING TO AN ORDER OF EXISTENCE
BEYOND THE VISIBLE OBSERVABLE UNIVERSE;
especially: OF OR RELATING TO GOD OR A GOD,
DEMIGOD, SPIRIT, OR DEVIL

2 A : DEPARTING FROM WHAT IS USUAL OR NORMAL ESPECIALLY SO AS TO APPEAR TO TRANSCEND THE LAWS OF NATURE. B : ATTRIBUTED TO AN INVISIBLE AGENT (AS A GHOST OR SPIRIT)

We live in a world that is filled with wondrous magical happenings each and every day. There's so much yet to be discovered. To be certain, delving into the unknown, the dark side, the "other side" has been around for centuries. Houdini—who, like Randi, had offered a reward to anyone who could prove he had supernatural powers—spent a good part of his life exposing charlatans who claimed they could communicate with the dead. Before he died, Houdini and his wife agreed on a secret password that Harry would use to let his bride know it was him should he be able to communicate after death. He did this because he knew that people would attempt to communicate with him after he died, and he was certain someone would step forward with a bogus claim. He was right. For years people attempted séances and readings. No one ever spoke or revealed the word Houdini's wife waited for: *believe. Believe* is such a powerful word.

People want to believe. They hope that death is not the end. They need to hold on to something bigger. It's human nature to do the least amount of work and want the biggest payoff. Las Vegas is a wonderful example of living that kind of hope-promise lifestyle. It's a city built on greed, fantasy, big dreams, and false hopes. Regardless of social or financial status, that mind-set of wanting more exists in everyone. Casinos are built on understanding human nature and the need and/or desire of never having enough and always wanting more. The house always wins because casinos play on instinct, weakness, and have the odds to their advantage. Eventually, you will lose. The psychology in setting up a billion-dollar hotel and casino also exists in the notion of magic. Each is carefully designed to make you believe that *anything* is possible.

147

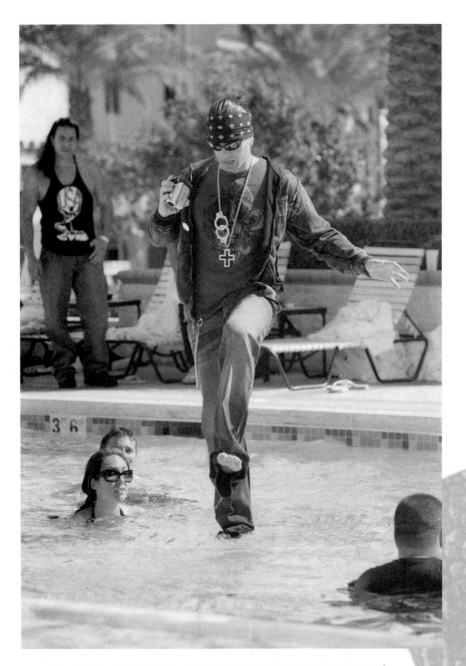

I'LL NEVER FORGET THE REACTIONS OF THE SPECTATORS AS I WALKED ON WATER, A DEMONSTRATION BROUGHT TO LIFE BECAUSE OF MY GUEST APPEARANCE ON NBC'S *Las Vegas*.

I believe impostors who masquerade as doing good are really doing great harm. They're con artists looking to take your money in exchange for false hope and dime-store trickery. As a young boy I was fascinated by trying to figure out things other people couldn't. I wanted a solution that could explain how something I thought was impossible became possible.

Today's society is full of promise for unsuspecting dupes. There are even psychic surgeons who claim to heal with psychic powers. The late, great comedian Andy Kaufman was so desperate for a cure to his cancer, he searched for alternative answers, including healing stones, transcendental meditation, and finally psychic surgery, which proclaimed the tumors could be removed from inside his body without making a visible incision. It's the oldest sleight-of-hand trick in the book. I've actually performed this demonstration on my television show using fake blood and chicken guts. It's unfortunate we live in a world where people buy into the notion that anything is possible . . . for a price. It's all a sham, and it makes me angry because I work so hard to entertain and bring joy to people's lives using many of the same techniques. I choose to use my skills in a positive way. If I were a man of fewer convictions, surely I'd be like all of these psychics pumping people for big bucks, swindling them of their hard-earned cash for my own good rather than risking my life on a regular basis in the name of art. I'd be one of the biggest names working as a spiritualist, making a fortune reading people's palms and talking to dead loved ones.

Those who take advantage of vulnerable people for cash are the scum of the earth. When I perform, I use my power, my gifts, my art to help people escape from the ordinary into the world of the extraordinary. I have the power to help them forget their problems, if only for a few moments. I find being able to give that to other people utterly intoxicating. I work hard to see my dreams and visions come to life. It's an honor and a great blessing to do what I do.

Much of what I do is innate; however, there are several techniques I have incorporated into my act as elements that can be used to create a large-scale demonstration. My act is who I am. I'm trying to create an experience that could be perceived as supernatural, unexplainable, otherworldly. I'm going to let you in on a little secret. Shhhh—don't tell anyone.

They're not.

People give off telltale signs without ever realizing they're feeding me the information I need to do the demonstration. I have the ability to allow people to feel in control when in reality, I'm always controlling them. Through body language, psychology, and verbal dialogue, most people will fall prey to what you want them to experience, which is the unexplainable.

This section of the book is a private, behind-the-scenes look at some of the methodology and process of creating my demonstrations and MINDFREAKs. When people perform these well, it appears so effortless. I want to show you how some of the process works and how a demonstration comes together so you can understand that these are not just tricks I make up and do the next day. There are a lot of elements that comprise the whole picture. Without perfection in each, the MINDFREAK would fail—and I would be busted.

MENTALISM

According to the encyclopedia, mentalism is an ancient performing art in which the practitioner uses mental acuity principles of stage magic and/or suggestions to present the demonstration or illusion of mind reading, psychokinesis, precognition, clairvoyance, or mind control.

Much of what I do incorporates principles of mentalism. Whether it's a trick using memory or mathematical equations, mentalism is magic with information. It looks very real. As a mentalist, I want you

MY FRIENDS BANACHECK, LANCE BURTON, AND JOHNNY THOMPSON
AFTER A VERY SUSPENSEFUL WINE BARREL DEMONSTRATION. AS
A MATTER OF FACT, IT WAS SO DANGEROUS LANCE OFFERED ME
MONEY TO NOT DO IT AGAIN.

to believe I can read your mind—hear your innermost thoughts. While I don't personally believe in psychic ability, a lot of people think a good mentalist possesses psychic skills. While I don't have any supernatural powers, I do have the power of observation. We all do. You just need to learn to tap into yours as I have done with mine.

I have had the privilege of working with one of the world's greatest mentalists, Banachek. Banachek is like my brother. He has been described as the cream of the crop when it comes to mentalism and is considered by most to be the world's greatest mentalist. In fact, he is the only mentalist ever to fool scientists into believing he possessed psychic powers. He is in the trenches with me every day. He's contributed a huge amount to making *MINDFREAK* a successful television series—and he does it all in the name of friendship.

If you asked me to read your mind right now, I might be able to make it appear as though I could, but in truth, I would really be reading your thoughts. Here's an easy way to understand what I mean. Let's say you're walking in the park and you see a husband and wife sitting on a park bench. A pretty girl walks by. The husband turns his head to look. The wife sees him. Would you know what each was thinking? Granted, that's a pretty obvious setup, but it's a great example of reading someone's thoughts. Given enough practice and information, I can take that art to the smallest level. There's a lot of psychology mixed in—and let's face it, a little trickery, too.

Psychology is one of the most important elements in practicing mentalism. I think the biggest difference between a magician and a mentalist is that a mentalist learns and understands psychology. Magicians might use elements of psychology, but they rarely understand it. Sometimes it's instinctive, but for many, it's a learning process and a continuous study of human psychology. Mentalism is often seen as a grown-up form of magic because it really speaks to the intellect as opposed to being about the illusion of pulling rabbits of out hats. Since I never wanted to be that kind of performer, I have learned to use mentalism to do some really amazing demonstrations. I've been fully blindfolded—unable to see a thing—and have safely driven Mandy Moore's BMW across Los Angeles. I have played a form of mental roulette with Korn's lead singer, Jonathan Davis, which was banned by the network for being extremely dangerous and too controversial. The network felt people would try to copy my demonstration and get hurt or even worse, killed. Each of these demonstrations uses various methods of mentalism that take years of practice to master.

There are a lot of myths surrounding mentalism and the realities of its existence. You cannot achieve superpowers by using any of these techniques. You can give the illusion of having some kind of supernatural gift, but you will probably never speak to your dead grandfather or make contact with the other side because paranormal activity is not real. There are a million scams out there contradicting what I just said, but the truth is, they are sophisticated schemes designed to take your money. Stay away from these types of false promises.

INTUITION

Intuition is defined as "that ability of the mind to develop answers to questions without consciously dealing with the problem at hand."

Instinct and intuition are both inherent traits. Some people claim that intuition is an aspect of the paranormal or psychic realm. Since I don't believe in either, it's hard for me to connect intuition to anything

WITH MY GOOD FRIENDS JONATHAN DAVIS AND MONKEY AT KORN STUDIOS IN BETWEEN TAKES FOR MY 2005 A&E HALLOWEEN SPECIAL.

other than a natural instinct one has. Have you ever had a feeling that you shouldn't take a particular flight or maybe you once started walking down a street and just sensed something wasn't right and turned around? That is intuition. It's learning to listen to your inner voice, which tells you to do or not do certain things. It's a bit like street smarts.

Intuition is an incredible resource and gift that we have been given to help us live the best life. Unfortunately, not many people know what it is or how to use it. The word *intuition* is Latin for "in to you." Theologian Florence Scovel Shinn said, "Intuition is the spiritual faculty that doesn't explain; it seemingly points the way." It's also been said that intuition is your divine spirit talking to you. If you will stop for a moment and acknowledge this, you will begin to realize the incredible perspective you have at your fingertips. You already have this very amazing power! And you don't even have to get any special training to start using it. All you need to do is raise your awareness about it and set your intention to harness it.

Intuitive messages range from an inkling to a strong sign or message. Your inner self is persistent and consistent. It will keep trying to get your attention until you finally wise up! An "inkling" is like a glimmer or passing feeling or thought that comes from somewhere inside and usually precedes a hunch or intuitive message. A "hunch" is accurate information from a higher intelligence; therefore, you can rely on it. Intuitive messages range from hearing actual words to seeing a clear picture or having a deep inner knowing. Some people experience intuition as a feeling, others as a gut reaction; some see images or have a dream, others hear an actual message, sometimes right and sometimes wrong. You can become more familiar with how your inner self communicates by learning to listen to your thoughts.

HYPNOSIS

Hypnosis is formally defined as "a psychological condition in which an individual may be induced to show apparent differences in behavior and thinking. It is a state of guided relaxation and focused attention." To me, it's more a game of suggestion. In this state of heightened awareness, positive suggestions easily and naturally achieve results and goals. Hypnosis is not sleep, but it gives a person the feeling of deep relaxation while remaining fully aware of what is going on.

Suggestive hypnotherapy uses the power of suggestion and is the mainstay of stage hypnosis. Stage hypnosis, when it's done well, is very effective. When it's done poorly, it can be horrific. The success of all hypnosis relies heavily on using a willing participant—it's critical to the outcome. Sheer willingness to volunteer is a sure sign that the person will go along with whatever suggestion I may make during a show. The participant and I essentially agree to play a game onstage together. To be clear, the hypnotic trance is neither a sleep state nor an unconscious state. The participant is fully aware of what is happening and is making a conscious decision to act out on suggestions I provide. The participant essentially assumes the pose that he feels is required in the hypnotic state. Therefore, if I suggest that someone is getting sleepy, they will feel like they're asleep and unconscious or anything else I lead them to believe they should feel. To the participant, this hypnotic state is very real.

My demonstrations always involve real people—not "stooges," or people I have planted in the audience. A good hypnotist has conviction in what he's doing. Your level of confidence and follow-through make all the difference in the world when it comes to effective stage hypnosis. No two people react the same way, so while I may get the same result, the show is always entertaining. There are usually three

A SUBLIMINAL HYPNOTIC DEMONSTRATION PERFORMED IN THE
STREETS OF LAS VEGAS DURING SEASON TWO.

types of people I deal with when selecting a participant. First, there's the very willing participant who came to see me hoping he'd be selected. Second, there's the wise guy who wants to prove he can't be hypnotized. Third, there's the person who simply wants to enjoy the show. It's up to me to select the right candidate. While I give the illusion that I am controlling the subject, the reality is, no one is ever fully out of control. The participant chooses to cooperate by willingly taking my suggestions.

Like all areas of mentalism, hypnosis relies on the use of psychology and an understanding of human behavior. Hypnosis may be induced in a disguised fashion so that a person doesn't realize they're being hypnotized. If I'm doing a mass-scale hypnosis demonstration, I might incorporate trance music, which mixes many methods to create a euphoric sensation when listened to. By hiding certain triggers within what seems to be a normal song, it is possible to create a long-lasting trancelike state in a person. Essentially, because of my musical ability, I have created "hypnosis" songs by mixing various psychological techniques within my music. Songs might include subliminal messages, relaxation methods, visualization and focus techniques, or bold psychological direction. The outcome is that person will be guided into hypnosis without being aware that the condition they're in *is* hypnosis.

ILLUSION

An illusion is defined as a general impression that does not correspond to actual fact. The human mind is designed to see things in patterns. The job of an illusionist is to fool you so that you don't see the patterns. If he's successful, there is no logical explanation other than what you just saw must be real, even though your mind is telling you it's impossible. Everything inside of you says it's real, but your mind tries to convince you it can't be, creating an internal conflict. A good illusionist is masterful at creating this internal conflict, but in a pleasant, entertaining way. It's entertainment, not confusion or frustration.

The mind is also designed to take shortcuts. Every time you look at something simple like a table, you don't process what it was before you came to the conclusion that it's a table because you use your previous experience to know and acknowledge you're seeing a table. If I were to cut that table in half, making it lighter and smaller, and perhaps make it into something on the other side, you still might conclude that it's just a table. An illusionist takes great advantage of his audience. He is hoping you will draw certain conclusions, having based your percep-

I LOOK AT THIS PICTURE AND WONDER WHY IN HELL I EVER
DECIDED TO DO THIS DEMONSTRATION.

tions on previous experiences. An illusion exploits the way you visually
process something. It can involve working with various dimensions,
angles, height, and depth perception. Your eyes fool your mind. What
appears to be a straight line can be a jagged path of twists and turns.
What appears to be one simple move can sometimes be the combination of fifty or more all at the same time.

An illusion is a highly choreographed collection of effects designed
to sell truth as well as deception. A single word can blow an entire effect. Much like writing music, the ultimate job of an illusionist is to
create a composition from all of these different parts so that they come
together in an arrangement that is symphonic and complete. When you
listen to a song, you aren't breaking down each sound, every instru-
ment, the singer, the background singers, and the mix. You just listen to
the song as a complete experience. That's the art of illusion.

The best performers have concepts, whether musicians or magicians.

They have a fully executed plan to arrange things in a particular order to work in tandem—in harmony—with one another. My musical background has given me a tremendous advantage in creating a demonstration, understanding its composition, and seeing it come together from inception through execution. Utilizing these various subgenres helps create more sophisticated and original material, using all forms of technology to bring the art into the day and age that we live in. Hopefully what I do amazes the audience. I want the audience to feel like they're an integral part of the event. Without them, I cannot do what I do.

CRISS JUMPS FROM A MOVING PRISONER TRANSPORT VEHICLE
BEFORE IT FALLS OVER A CLIFF WHILE SHOOTING SEASON THREE.

Chapter Ten

Believe

Laying on a bed of nails while trying to hold one-quarter of a Hummer's weight as it drives across my chest.

As a species, we're programmed from a very young age to get what we want. When a baby cries, he gets a bottle. When a little kid throws a temper tantrum, he gets a toy. A lot of parents would rather pacify a child than take the time to discipline him. Life doesn't always work the way you want it to. You have to work hard to achieve the things you want. I'm somebody who has always known what I want. From the simplest things, like a certain effect, to the more complex, like crafting an entire episode for my television show—deciding what it's about, where it should take place, when it should be shot, and so on—I know the image in my mind and can precisely execute that thought or idea into becoming something real.

Achieving success is incredibly difficult. It is a painstaking commitment that requires sacrifice and passion. I have literally given my blood, sweat, and tears to achieve my goals and to have the kind of success I dreamed about as a boy. I'm not saying I'm better than anyone else, but I definitely know myself better than anyone else. I know I work harder than anyone else. When you work really hard, your sense of pride in everything you do is greater. You value your accomplishments and cherish the feeling that you get what you deserve and shouldn't feel guilty about reaping the rewards for all of that hard work. There's a level appreciation for it that can only be achieved through determined discipline and dedication.

My father always told me, "What you can dream is what you can get if you're willing to go through whatever it takes to get it." He said, "Son, you have to always be realistic and let your actions speak louder than your words."

"I worried about my son when he told me he wanted to be a professional magician. I wanted him to become a doctor or a lawyer. But I recognized that **Christopher was special** at a very early age. He had a passion for magic. When your child comes to you and tells you what they want to be, as a parent you have to support your child. Talk to them. Help them to understand the commitment it takes *to pursue their dreams* and then **do whatever you can to help them achieve them**. That's what my husband and I did for all of our children."

Dimitra, my mom

I think of myself as a ninja in every area of my life. I am laser-focused on achieving my goals. If doors are closed, I figure out a way to swing opportunities wide open—whether I have to climb through the window or come out of a vent. There's always a way in if you want it bad enough. There's a way to achieve your dreams for each of you. It's

a matter of analyzing them, being methodical, and putting forth the effort, time, and commitment to making them happen.

You also have to learn to become a great problem solver. You can solve any challenge if you think clearly, look at a situation head-on, and prioritize solutions. That's how I deal with things. Unfortunately, I sometimes fall at the bottom of that priority list, which means there are times where my personal life suffers. I've stayed laser-focused on achieving success, sometimes to the detriment of my family. This is a regret. But it is who I am, and for the moment anyway, this is how I need to live my life.

I'd like to find a better balance, but in the midst of all the chaos that surrounds my crazy, hectic *MINDFREAK* world, fair—and even balance—is not an option. Though I know it will be someday, it's not where I'm at right now. Sadly, it's the people I am closest to who are sometimes the sacrificial lambs because they are the people who unconditionally love and support me and my dreams. They know how hard I've worked to get here—writing a book, shooting a television show, recording a new album, building a permanent live show, living each and every day doing whatever it takes to turn my dreams into reality. At some point, there are just no more hours in the day to give.

"Criss and I were talking recently, REMINISCING ABOUT THE OLD DAYS of working in his parents' backyard talking about how one day, **he was going to make it big**. When I think about it, it wasn't that long ago, yet it has taken Criss fourteen years to get here. We were getting ready to shoot a **motorcycle jump** in the back of the Aladdin Hotel. Thousands of people were there to watch Criss work. This wasn't even a publicized event. IT WAS JUST ANOTHER DAY AT THE OFFICE FOR US. We're just now starting to realize that people have begun *to latch onto the dream*."

John Farrell, my production designer

Even though I've been chasing the dream for years, success is relatively new to me. There's so much to learn and maneuver—to confront and deal with so that I am doing the right things and making the best choices along the way. It's a juggling act, one I am still learning to get right. Success and failure both come with a price. I believe the real task is to figure out how to handle both in a way that serves me professionally *and* personally.

165

MY APPEARANCE IN THE MIDDLE OF MORE THAN TWO THOUSAND
PEOPLE AFTER THE MOTORCYCLE JUMP.

For most of my life, there has been no separation between my professional and personal lives. They've always been synonymous. I don't turn my phone off. I can be reached twenty-four/seven because I work twenty-four/seven. Everything I am working toward requires me to be available and reachable. I don't have two weeks off for a vacation. I don't get sick pay. I've never had that kind of job. I have built a business that operates around the clock seven days a week, three hundred sixty-five days a year.

It has never been a question of *if* success would happen but rather, *when* it would happen. The unconditional love and support from my family have been critical to my success. No matter how often I failed, I never failed in my family's eyes. They were always there to give me a pep talk, to give me the freedom to create, explore, experiment, and to aim for this crazy dream. I am incredibly grateful for the opportunities I've had in my life, but from the inside looking out, I've created a very large, sometimes scary beast of an operation that is vastly multidimensional and the best thing that has ever happened in my life. I love it. I thrive on it. I wouldn't know how to live any other way.

Epilogue

MINDFREAK LIVE— THE NEXT CHAPTER

While season two of *MINDFREAK* was amazing, season three has given me the opportunity to accomplish many dreams. First and foremost, by the end of the season, I will have created and filmed more than seventy half-hour episodes of magic for television, which is a pretty amazing accomplishment in and of itself. Season three has brought me to a higher professional place to work side by side with some of the finest experts in television. We've become a well-oiled machine. Things have calmed down a little since season one. I no longer go out there and risk my life in every episode. I'm grateful for that! (So is my family.)

When we first began filming the original episodes of *MINDFREAK*, we were lucky if fifteen people showed up to see what we were doing. Now, thousands show up when the cameras begin to roll. The allegiance and dedication from you, the Loyal, hasn't gone unnoticed or without deep gratitude.

Now that there's a familiarity with my art and for many of you, with me personally, the potential to grow as a performer has exponentially increased. I'm having a lot of fun trying to incorporate some of that intimacy in the new demonstrations, as well as my exciting new live show projected to open at our new home, the Luxor Hotel, in spring 2008. Season three isn't just about what demonstration I'm doing, but how we get there too. I'm using my celebrity to engage the viewing audience in a different way than I could have in previous seasons. Now that people have a sense of what I'm all about, I can open myself up and show people who Criss Angel really is. Much of that has to do with revealing the real me—Christopher from Long Island—and learning to just be myself. My personality can shine through during my performance, which allows the entire experience to become even more organic than it could ever have been during my first season on *MINDFREAK*. Season one was all about being precise and specific. I had a need to draw the audience in by doing mind-blowing demonstrations every show. So, that's why season one was filled with provocative feats of endurance like flying by fishhooks or lighting myself on fire. Each week was about whether I would live or die. I had to get people interested in me as a performer before I could expect anyone to care about me on a personal or intimate level as an artist.

I worked so hard to create the buzz of "who is this guy?" and "why is he doing this?" Season two gave me the chance to be a little more diverse, doing demonstrations like floating from one building to another, making a nine-thousand-pound elephant disappear in the street, and taking six celebrities to a purportedly paranormal location in Death Valley, capturing some of the most insane events ever filmed. We were able to show people that my art isn't one-dimensional.

I never want you to know what to expect from me. That's why season three expands into more personal dimensions. I can show who I am through my personality and people will be engaged with watching it because they feel like they know me. Season three is about diversity and experimentation. I've changed my look a little, cut my hair shorter than it has been in years. I'm consciously changing everything I can to

keep evolving as a person and performer. When people come up and ask for an autograph, we're using that moment as an opportunity to break into a demonstration. My art speaks for itself. It is an extension of who I am, but it doesn't define me. If I ever feel like I don't have anything else to say artistically, I won't do this anymore. So far, thankfully, that isn't the case.

The highlight of *MINDFREAK* season three involves the most insane levitation of all time. Every year, the number one request from people is to see me levitate. People seem really fascinated and engaged with the idea of zero gravity and flying. So every season, I try to come up with the most provocative, engaging, incredible insane demonstrations on the art of levitation. This year is bigger and better than ever. I will literally float four hundred plus feet in the air in the light that emanates from the top of the Luxor Hotel above Las Vegas Boulevard. For those of you who aren't familiar, the Luxor Hotel in Las Vegas is an architectural wonder. It is an actual glass pyramid. There are only a couple manmade things on earth that can be seen from outer space. One is the Great Wall of China, and another is the Luxor Light. It will be the biggest and brightest spotlight any performer could dream of ever being seen in. I recently climbed to the top of the hotel, climbed off the balcony at the pinnacle, and began to float from the balcony of the top floor inside the pyramid to the atrium level. It was insane—even for me. It was by far one of the most outrageous demonstration I have ever done.

The challenge to pull off these demonstrations grows with increased technology. Even more so now that people recognize me. I have to legitimately accomplish what I set out to do in one take, with a live audience monitoring my every move. Everyone has cameras and cell phones, so if I make one mistake it's captured. I am willing to risk my reputation every time. I'm challenged by the idea of what I have to lose and confident enough in my skill that I can rise to the occasion. I employ technology and different skills that allow me to do demonstrations that no other magician has ever been able to do in the world, especially in public forums such as the Luxor Hotel.

If I fail at any demonstration, it would be exposed on the Internet within minutes. That challenge keeps things interesting for me—it keeps me real. My motivation has always been to be the guy who raises the bar in magic. I know I have contributed a tremendous amount in terms of creatively changing and reinventing the art.

"*Women flock to him.*
Guys want to HANG OUT WITH HIM.
As long as he's nice to kids and pets,
he can't fail!"

*Felix Rappaport, president and COO,
Luxor Las Vegas Casino Hotel*

All of this attention has taken some getting used to. I am so grateful for the experiences, but it has been an enormous adjustment to suddenly find myself in the tabloids for who I'm dating, especially when I worked so hard to keep my personal life private. My newfound celebrity has its perks too. I recently got pulled over for running a red light (I won't say in what city). It was completely my fault. When I opened the door of my lambo the officers were shocked to see me step out of the car. We chatted for a few minutes, I offered to have the two cops come down for a taping of *MINDFREAK*, and before I knew it, no ticket. I'm not sure I could have gotten away with that a few years ago!

I'm perpetually late these days because it takes me an extra twenty minutes to greet the people who wait for me to walk in or out of the Luxor Hotel while we shoot season three. No matter how successful I become, I will always make it a point to take whatever time is needed to interact with those people because without them, I wouldn't have a career. I appreciate those moments. They keep me grounded, and though my ego is never satisfied, I never want it to get too out of check to not stop and say hello. Although I have to admit, it completely freaked me out when Ron Woods of the Rolling Stones e-mailed me to say he's a big fan. He wanted to invite me to the Stones concert in Vegas. It was insane.

As I put the final touches on this book, I thought back to the first time I came to Las Vegas ten years ago. I was driving the cheapest rental car I could find down the strip, dreaming how someday I would be headlining in Vegas like Siegfried and Roy and Lance Burton. I fantasized about my own marquee, my name up there in lights. I had nothing but my belief in myself and my dream. How incredible, how sweet it is to be in Vegas today, overlooking the same boulevard of dreams from a decade ago, knowing my fantasy has become a reality. I pinch myself all the time. It wasn't so long ago I was driving that rental car and staying in a $39-a-night hotel room looking for work on the strip. I remain eternally grateful for the love and support of my family, for their tenacity to ride this crazy roller coaster with me every day. People

doubted me, promised me, and never kept their word. For years, I heard empty promises of what someone could do for me. In the end, it's all bullshit. You have to go out there and make your own way in life. It doesn't get any sweeter than working hard for something and having it pay off. The more you have at risk, the bigger it pays. And when it pays big, it's amazing.

Be careful what you wish for . . .

CRISS WITH SELECT CARS AND MOTORCYCLES FROM HIS COLLECTION
AT THE *DUB* MAGAZINE SHOOT OF JUNE 2007.

Part II

40 MINDFREAKS

Criss Angel and Richard Kaufman

Photographs by Pete Biro

PERFORMING YOUR OWN MINDFREAKS

Introduction

Magicians have beaten the hell out of the magic. I never want to become so jaded and lose my innocence to the art of magic because of the crap that's out there. Perhaps the forty MINDFREAKS I teach in this section of the book will bring you back to the joy and excitement of performing magic or introduce you to it for the first time. There are forty beginner and intermediate level tricks that you can easily perform, each with a cool sensibility. I want people to fall in love with the art, to get bitten by the bug like I did when I was a kid. If this book bridges the gap between old-school and contemporary magic, that would be a wonderful gift. Have fun with it. It's a wonderful skill to be able to entertain, confuse, and present magic to a group of people. It enables you to not only think about what you're doing in that moment but to also effectively deal and interact with people.

For a moment of magic to work, you have to implement a series of actions for that moment of awe, that inevitable "How did you do that?" moment. To do this, you must get very good at distracting or misdirecting your audience. While talking about what you're about to do or what you're doing at that very moment, you're really setting up and presetting the big payoff. You know you have to secretly hit a button, get something out of your pocket, put something up your sleeve, or get your audience to look at your left hand so they don't see what you're doing with your right. You have to get to a point where those moves are so comfortable, they're second nature.

There's an inherent danger to magic when the presentation quality of a performer is inadequate. A trick can be good on its own. Anyone can do the tricks I've provided in the "40 MINDFREAKS" section. The tricks will amaze your friends . . . but will you? Will your audience only remember the trick or will they also remember the performer who did this amazing trick? A really good performer gets a reaction for the effect as well as the execution. I can't tell you how many times I've been to magic clubs, sat in the audience, watched an amateur magician do his thing, and later overheard audience members talking about what an amazing trick they saw but having no clue about who performed the mind-blowing demonstration. An audience should walk out the door remembering the performer *and* the trick.

Have fun, practice often, put your own twist on things to make these your very own, and, by all means, keep reaching for your dreams.

Practice Tips

Remember that magic is only as good as your presentation—the way you behave and talk when presenting an effect. If you don't put ample time into practicing your presentation, you won't create strong magic.

Once you have learned an effect you must, like an athlete, run through the technique and visualize your performance over and over again in your mind.

At the same time, practice in front of a mirror and/or videotape your performance to see what it looks like from a spectator's perspective. Once you have mastered it, perform it for family, friends, and *then* strangers. This is the process I personally use from the moment of creation to final performance.

Enjoy, you MINDFREAK!

Criss Angel

MINDFREAKS
CONTENTS

1.

DISSOLVING GLASS

Criss will cause a coin to pass through the table. First, he wraps a glass in a paper napkin so the people cannot see through it, and then he covers the coin with the wrapped glass. Unfortunately, the coin refuses to pass through the table—instead, the glass vanishes.

To Prepare

You need a small drinking glass, a paper napkin, and you must sit at a table opposite everyone else.

To Perform

Borrow a quarter from someone and place it on the table, about a foot away from your edge, tails side up. Say, *"I will make the coin pass through the table magically—solid through solid, matter through matter."*

Open the napkin once (so it's still folded in half) and lay it on the table. Turn the glass on its side, with the open end toward you, and place it at one end of the napkin. Roll the napkin around the glass (photo 1), keeping the bottom edge of the napkin in line with the edge of the glass (photo 2). Stand the wrapped glass

upright. Now twist the portion of the napkin that extends past the top of the glass (photo 3). The napkin now forms a "shell" over the glass.

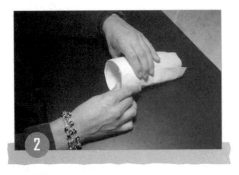

Make sure that the napkin is not folded too tightly—the glass must be able to slide *easily* in and out.

Say, *"I have to cover the coin with this glass so that you won't see the hole in the table open up when the coin goes through. Some people go crazy when they see the hole in the table."* Place the covered glass over the coin, mouth down (photo 4).

Snap your fingers and announce that the coin has passed through the table. Lift the glass with your right hand—the coin will still be on the table. Say, *"That's strange, I don't know why it didn't work."* Replace the glass over the coin, covering it.

Again snap your fingers and announce that the coin has passed through the table. Lift the glass with your right hand—the coin is still there. Now say, *"I know—the coin needs to be heads side up!"* Your right hand lifts the glass and moves inward to the edge of the table while your left hand *simultaneously* moves outward to pick up the coin (photo 5).

While everyone is watching your left hand turn the coin over, your right hand relaxes its grip on the napkin just enough to allow the glass to silently slide out and into your lap (photo 6 is an exposed view). Make sure that the lower edge of the napkin is *beneath the table edge* at that moment so nobody sees the glass fall. If you have rolled the glass in the napkin correctly, it will slide out with no trouble. If it won't come out, then you probably rolled the napkin around the glass too tightly (or you are holding it too tightly with your hand).

The instant the glass is gone, your right hand moves forward and covers the coin with the napkin "shell," which will look as if the glass is still under it. You can set the napkin "shell" on the table over the coin and move both hands away—it won't fall over.

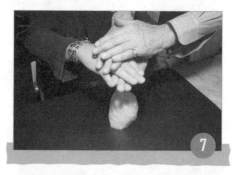

Hold both your hands, palm down, a few inches above the napkin. Ask someone to put his hands on top of yours (photo 7). Quickly pull your hands out from under his hands and, before he can do any-

thing, put your hands *on top of his* (photo 8) and push them downward so they crush the napkin "shell"—the glass has vanished (photo 9).

Do not bring the glass out from under the table—leave it "vanished"! You'll have plenty of time later on (perhaps as you're leaving) to sneak the glass out of your lap and back onto the table.

2. ~

LEVITATING ROLL

Criss shows both sides of a napkin, which he holds in front of himself. Suddenly a mysterious shape appears behind the napkin and pushes it forward. After a moment, a dinner roll floats up from behind the napkin and dances around—then it vanishes and the napkin may be examined.

To Prepare

You need a napkin, a fork, and the object you want to make appear and float—in this case it's a dinner roll. You must sit at a table opposite everyone. Secretly, under cover of the table, push the prongs of the fork into the side of the dinner roll (photo 1) and put the whole thing in your lap so the handle of the fork is to the right (photo 2).

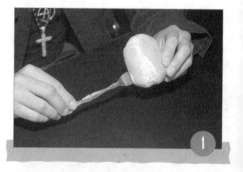

To Perform

Unfold the napkin completely and show both sides. Lay it flat on the table so that a bit of it hangs over the table edge, near you.

Show your hands empty, then let them drop into your lap as you say, *"I'm going to show you something fantastic."*

As you speak, your right hand grasps the end of the fork between your thumb and first finger. Grasp the inner left corner of the napkin with your left hand (photo 3). Lift your right hand up behind the napkin and grasp its inner right corner between the back of your first finger and your second finger (photo 4).

Now raise both hands straight up so the napkin hangs downward with the fork and dinner roll hidden behind it (photo 5 is what the audience sees).

You'll find that your right thumb and first finger can easily control the movements of the dinner roll with the end of the fork they hold. Push the dinner roll forward so everyone sees a bump appear in the center of the napkin (photo 6). Then, move the dinner roll around a little, swinging it back and forth so the bump appears, disappears, and moves around.

Eventually, raise the dinner roll so it's visible to everyone, peeking over the top of the napkin (photo 7)—it should sit right on the upper edge of the napkin—you don't want to expose the fork (photo 8 is an exposed view).

After a moment, lower the dinner roll down so it moves behind the napkin again. The bottom edge of the napkin should be draped behind the edge of the table so no one can see under it. Simply let go of the fork—the dinner roll and fork together will fall into your lap (photo 9), unseen by everyone but you.

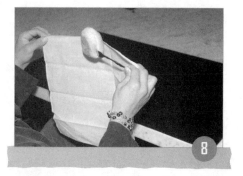

Quickly crumple the napkin into a ball and throw it on the table to end the mystery.

3. ~

PRECOGNITION

There are five objects on the table: a cup, a paper napkin, a straw, a fork, and a sugar packet. Criss writes a secret prediction on a piece of paper, folds it in half, and places it in someone's pocket. Criss and that person take turns eliminating the objects on the table in a game of chance until only one object remains—the fork. When the person reads the paper that he has in his pocket, he sees that Criss has correctly predicted the future by writing: "The Fork Will Be Left."

To Prepare

You can use any five objects. In this case, let's assume you use a cup, a paper napkin, a straw, a fork, and a sugar packet. You also need a sheet of blank paper and a pen.

To Perform

Write "The Fork Will Be Left" on the paper. Don't let anyone else see what you've written. Fold the paper in half so the prediction is on the inside and give it to someone to hold. Ask him to place it in his pocket so he can't peek before the end of the experiment.

Ask the same person to help you. Say, *"We'll take turns at this game."* Cover any two of the five objects on the table, one with each hand, *but do not cover the fork.* (The secret to this trick is simple: NEVER cover the item that you've written as your prediction—in this case the fork.) Let's assume that you cover the straw and the sugar packet. Say, *"You can tell me to discard either one of the objects I've chosen."* Let's assume that he tells you to get rid of the straw—place it aside.

Tell him to cover any two objects; assume he covers the cup and fork. You must tell him to discard the cup because you want the fork to remain. If he does not cover the fork, then you can tell him to discard either object—it doesn't matter. In this way the fork never gets taken away; *you* will never cover it, so he cannot tell you to discard it, and if he covers it, you will always tell him to get rid of the *other* item.

So far he has told you to get rid of the straw, and you have told him to discard the cup. Now you must cover two more objects. Since there are only three left, and you can't cover the fork, you must cover the sugar packet and the napkin. He tells you to discard one of them—say it's the napkin.

He covers the two remaining objects. Since you want the fork to remain, you instruct him to discard the sugar packet.

The fork will remain on the table. Say, *"Did I influence you in any way? You could have chosen any objects at any time. Get ready for a miracle. Please read my prediction."*

When he takes out the piece of paper and reads "The Fork Will Remain," everyone will be dumbfounded—and might even think you can predict the future.

4. ⚊

SIXTH SENSE

Criss unfolds a paper napkin and tears it into nine square pieces, each about the same size. He picks one piece randomly and gives it to a woman who's watching. She takes a red marker and signs her name on it while Criss uses a black marker to sign his name on the other eight pieces. Then, all the pieces are mixed together and given to Criss behind his back. Without looking, he picks out the one piece on which the spectator has signed her name.

To Prepare
You need a paper napkin, a black marker, and a red marker.

To Perform
Unfold the napkin and show that it is completely unprepared and blank on both sides.

Next, tear the napkin into nine approximately square pieces (photo 1). This is easy to do: first tear the napkin into three approximately equal strips, then tear those strips into three approximately equal squares.

When you're tearing the napkin, keep track of the center piece—it is the only one with torn edges on all *four* sides. This is how you will locate it later.

Once you have the nine pieces, pick the center piece out of the bunch (as if it is a random choice) and give it to a woman in the audience along with the red marker.

Ask her to sign her name on the piece she holds while you quickly sign (or initial) the other eight pieces.

When all the pieces have been signed, mix them together and give all nine back to the woman who is helping you. Tell her that she may mix up the pieces some more if she wishes.

Turn your back and ask the woman to hand the pieces to you, behind your back. Now turn and face her.

Begin feeling the edges of each piece of napkin until you find one (there is only one) that has four rough edges. It is the piece she has signed in red marker. Once you've found it, bring it out front and hold it up so everyone can see her signature in red. Crumple all the other pieces in a ball and toss them away.

5. ⬤

LOST AND FOUND

Criss has two cards chosen from the deck. These cards are "lost" in two different parts of the deck. Suddenly, as the deck is tossed from one hand to the other, Criss plucks the two cards from the deck—the chosen cards.

To Prepare

You need an ordinary deck of playing cards. Remove the following cards: the eight of spades, the eight of clubs, the seven of hearts, and the seven of diamonds.

Place the seven of diamonds on the bottom of the deck. Arrange the other three cards on top of the deck in this order, from top down: eight of spades, seven of hearts, eight of clubs. The eight of spades should be on top of the deck.

To Perform

The first thing you must do is to "force" someone to take the top two cards of the deck: the eight of spades and seven of hearts. Be cool

and it'll be easy to do. Hand the
deck to a person and say, *"Please
cut off a small group of cards from
the top of the deck and flip them
faceup back onto the deck."* (Photo
1 shows what happens.) Once the
spectator has followed your instructions, continue, *"Now please
cut deeper, so you are taking off a
larger group of cards, and flip all
of them over, back onto the deck."*
(Photo 2 shows the result and how
the deck is arranged at this point:
there is a small group of faceup
cards on top, followed by the rest
of the deck, facedown. The cards
that were originally on top of the

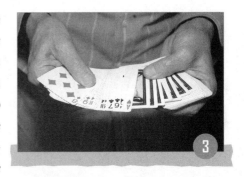

deck are now on top of the facedown portion. *Note:* The deck is *not*
actually spread at this point—the photo is posed this way *only* to show
you the condition of the cards.)

Take the deck back and spread the cards between your hands until
you come to the first facedown card (photo 3). Remove all the faceup
cards from the top. Square them into a neat pile, turn them facedown,
and place them on the table. Say, *"Let's use the first two facedown
cards."* Your right hand removes the first two facedown cards from the
deck in your left hand and shows them to the person (photo 4) as you
say, *"A red seven and a black eight."* Do *not* mention the suits!

Place the red seven (hearts) and the black eight (spades) on top of
the facedown packet of cards on the table. Ask the person to cut the
packet, burying his two cards in its center.

Your right hand lifts about half of the cards in your left hand. Ask the person to pick up the packet from the table and place it on top of the cards, which remain in your left hand. Now, you drop the cards held by your right hand on top. To the spectator, it seems as if the two cards he randomly chose have been completely lost in the center of the deck.

Take the squared deck with your right hand, holding it with your thumb on top and fingers beneath (photo 5). You'll have to practice what happens next a few times so you know exactly how loosely to hold the cards. Swing your right hand to the left, pressing your right thumb and fingers lightly together. The deck should fly into your left hand, slipping out from between the top and bottom cards (photo 6 shows this just starting), which remain in your right hand.

Your left hand catches the deck (photo 7). Turn your right hand over to reveal what seem to be the same two cards you placed in the deck a moment ago—a red seven and a black eight (photo 8). Wait a few moments for the trick to register, then insert the two cards in different places in the deck and shuffle the cards. Keeping them in sight for too long at the end of the trick may provide someone in the audience with the opportunity to remember that the suits are different.

6. —

TOGETHER TORN

Five cards are randomly chosen from a deck of playing cards and torn in half by Criss. No matter how often the spectator wishes the performer to mix the halves, the matching halves of each card always find each other.

To Prepare
You need an old deck of playing cards that you can destroy.

To Perform
Give the deck to someone who's watching and ask that he or she remove any five cards. Once they have been removed, place the rest of the deck aside—it won't be used again.

Hold all five cards squarely together and facedown. Tear them all in half widthwise (photo 1).

Take the half-cards held by your right hand and place them on the table to your right.

Deal the half-cards that remain in your left hand onto the table into a pile one at a time, secretly reversing their order. This second pile should be to the left of the first one (photo 2).

To the spectator who first selected the five cards, say, *"We're going to play a little game called `Will the Cards Match?' I am going to spell*

out each of the words in the phrase
'Will the Cards Match?' and at any
time you may tell me to switch
packets—right in the middle of
spelling the word! In fact, it's more
amazing the more often you ask me
to switch. Also, at the beginning of
each word, you tell me which packet
to start spelling with."

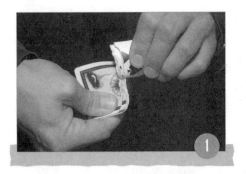

Ask the person to point to either
packet, and pick up the one she indicates. Begin to spell "W-I-L-L." For
each letter that you say, take the top
card off and put it on the bottom of
the packet. A half-card is transferred
from top to bottom for each letter.

Make sure she understands that she can tell you to switch packets at any
time. If she does tell you to switch, simply put down the packet you're
holding and pick up the other one. Then continue to spell the word, beginning with the letter after the one she stopped you on in the other packet.
In other words, if she stopped you after "W-I," then you would resume
spelling by saying "L-L." Remember to transfer a card from top to bottom for each letter. It does not matter if she never tells you to switch, or
asks you to switch packets on every letter. After you've finished spelling,
place the packet you're still holding on the table.

Take the top half-card off of each packet and place them together in
a separate spot on the table, away from both packets.

Repeat the entire business again, this time spelling the word
"T-H-E." At the conclusion you will place a second pair of half-cards on
the table off by themselves.

Repeat the entire business again, this time spelling the word "C-A-R-D-S." At the conclusion you will place a third pair of half-cards on the table off by themselves.

Repeat the entire business again, this time spelling the word "M-A-T-C-H." At the conclusion you will place a fourth pair of half-cards on the table off by themselves.

You will be left with a single half-card from each packet—pair these together on the table.

Say, *"Do the cards match . . . of course!"* Turn over the pairs of half-cards one at a time to reveal that all the halves have found their proper matching mates (photo 3).

7. ⟶

PREMONITION

Criss writes a prediction on a piece of paper and folds it in half. Different people call out various colors, and the magician writes each color that has been mentioned on a different slip of paper. Each slip is folded in half and dropped into a small box or paper bag. One person is allowed to freely pick any one of the folded slips from the box. After he reads what color is written on it, Criss's prediction is also read—and they match!

To Prepare
You need a small box (such as a shoe box) or a plain paper bag. It must be opaque so that no one can see through it. You also need a small pad of paper and a pen or pencil.

To Perform
Say, *"I am going to predict the future on this piece of paper."* Write the word "RED" on one piece of paper, then fold it in half and give it to a person to hold—this is your prediction.

Ask someone else to call out the name of any color. Then, write the word "RED" on a piece of paper. This is a very clever swindle: ignore what the person has said and write "RED." The people watching will think that you are writing the name of the color that the volunteer has called out.

Fold the paper in half and drop it into the box or bag.

Repeat exactly the same con with other people who are watching, and each time a color is called out, write down "RED" on a different slip of paper. Each piece of paper is folded in half and dropped into the box or bag.

You should have at least five or six different colors chosen. The people now think there are five or six pieces of paper in the box, each with a different color written on it. Actually all of the pieces have the word "RED" written on them.

Here are a few tips: if no one calls out the color red, simply say, *"I will also choose some colors myself!"* Then, you write "RED" on two or three slips of paper and drop those into the box or bag.

Also, if someone calls out "purple," you must pretend to write for a bit longer than if someone calls out "red."

Ask someone to reach into the box and select any one of the pieces of paper. Have him unfold it and read the color aloud. Of course he will say "RED" because that is what is written on *every* piece!

Ask the person who is holding your prediction to read that, and he will also say "RED," proving that you have predicted in advance which color would be selected.

Put the box or bag containing the rest of the slips of paper away and begin your next trick.

Note that if someone does call out the color "RED," you can briefly display that word to everyone once you've written it on the paper.

8. ⟶

RESTORATION

Criss shows both sides of a paper napkin. He rips it into small pieces and then magically restores it to one whole piece.

To Prepare

You need two paper napkins. Open one of the napkins and crush it into a small ball. Hold this ball inside the curled third and fourth fingers of your right hand (photo 1). The ball should be hidden from view by the back of your hand, and the hand will look natural and not attract suspicion if you don't curl your fingers too tightly. It's important to keep your hand as relaxed as possible.

You also need a pen, pencil, or cigarette lighter in your right jacket or pants pocket.

To Perform

Take the other napkin and, using both hands, unfold it. Show both sides.

Tear the napkin in half straight down the center (photo 2). Put the pieces together (one

behind the other) and tear them in half again. Put the pieces together and tear them in half one more time.

Using the fingers of both hands, crush the torn pieces into a small ball. Hold this ball between your right thumb and first finger, in front of the hidden ball, which you've had in your hand the whole time (photo 3 is an exposed view).

Bring your hands together, palm to palm, as if to rub them against each other, rolling the paper into a ball between them. Now you will switch one ball for the other. When you first bring your hands together palm to palm, they will look like photo 4 (the hands are held slightly apart so you can see inside—the audience would not see this). The whole napkin is the one between your palms, closer to you. The torn napkin is the one between your fingers.

Curl your right fingers around the torn napkin ball so it is hidden inside them, then take the whole napkin ball with your left thumb and fingers (photo 5 is an exposed view). Immediately raise your left hand to your mouth and blow on the napkin it holds. At the same time your right hand (with the torn napkin ball hidden inside) drops to your side (photo 6).

Insert your right hand into the pocket containing the pen, pencil, or cigarette lighter. Leave the torn napkin in your pocket and bring out the other item. If it's a pen or pencil, use it like a magic wand and wave it over your left hand (photo 7). If it's a cigarette lighter, then ignite it and wave it around your left hand (at a safe distance). Either way put the object on the table afterward.

Now open your left hand—the napkin looks the same to the audience. Use both hands to open it up and reveal that it is completely restored to one piece (photo 8).

9. —

PROCREATION

Criss rips a napkin into pieces and makes three small balls out of it. He places two in his hand and one in his pocket. Faster than the eye can see, the third ball jumps back to his hand. This happens several times and the final time, when Criss opens his hand, dozens of tiny balls pop out.

To Prepare

You need about four napkins and you must be wearing a jacket or coat of some sort.

Take three of the napkins and tear each one into eight pieces of about equal size (most napkins are folded in quarters, so simply divide each quarter in half). Crumple the eight pieces from each napkin into separate little balls. When you've done this with all three napkins, you should have twenty-four little balls. Put all these little balls in your right jacket or coat pocket.

To Perform

Show the paper napkin and tear off three pieces, each about the same size as the pieces you used to make the little balls. Crush each piece into a ball—you should now have three more balls, each the same size as the ones in your pocket. Put the rest of the napkin aside. The only pieces of napkin that are now visible are the three little balls you've just made in front of the audience.

Give the three balls to some-one to look at for a moment. At the same time, your right hand sneaks into your right jacket or coat pocket and secretly steals *one* of the twenty-four little balls. Hold it inside your fingers by curling them a little—the people must not know this ball is hidden in your hand.

Say, *"I'm going to put two of these balls in my hand and one in my pocket."* Pick up one of the little balls with your right hand (photo 1 is an exposed view) and put it into your left hand. Pick up a second ball and also put it into your left hand, at the same time letting the extra ball drop with it (photo 2 is an exposed view, photo 3 is what the people watching actually see). It will look as if you have simply dropped two balls into your left hand, though there are actually three. Quickly close your left fingers when your right hand moves away.

Pick up the third ball with your right hand and put it in your pocket—only you actually keep the ball hidden inside your right fingers as before.

Ask, *"How many in my hand?"* Someone will say "Two." Open your left hand to reveal three balls! Turn your left hand over and dump the balls onto the table.

Repeat the entire business a second time. That is, put one ball into your left hand. As you put the second ball into your left hand, secretly

drop the third (hidden) ball in with it. Pick up the third ball with your right hand and actually conceal it in your hand as you pretend to place it in your pocket. Open your left hand to reveal that the third ball has jumped back.

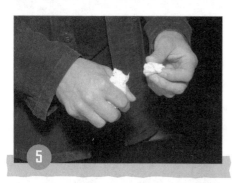

Repeat the entire business a third time. That is, put one ball into your left hand. As you put the second ball into your left hand, secretly drop the third (hidden) ball in with it. Pick up the third ball with your right hand and actually conceal it in your hand as you pretend to place it in your pocket. Open your left hand to reveal that the third ball has jumped back.

Now, you should have done something a little differently that last time: when your right hand enters your pocket, instead of simply concealing the single ball in your hand, grab as many of the twenty-four little balls as possible and close your hand around them (photo 4 is an exposed view). It doesn't matter if you don't get all of them.

When you bring your right hand out of your pocket, all eyes will be on your left hand because you've programmed the people watching to look there at this moment, so don't worry. Open your left hand and show three balls again.

Say, *"I'll do it a little differently this last time. Perhaps it would be easier to follow if I put the balls in my right hand."* Your left hand puts two of the balls, one at a time, into your right hand (photo 5). You must be careful here not to expose all the little balls yet. Your left hand can poke the balls in through the top of your fist.

Now, your *left* hand takes the third ball and places it into your *left* jacket pocket. Ask someone how many balls are in your right hand. No matter what he or she says, open your right hand and let all the balls pop out for a surprise ending (photo 6).

10 . —

LINKED

Criss lays a piece of string on the table, then covers its center with a handkerchief. He borrows a finger ring from someone who's watching, then he places the finger ring, and a small safety pin, under the handkerchief. The ends of the string remain in full view at all times, yet Criss magically links the finger ring onto the string.

To Prepare
You need a piece of string, a handkerchief, and a small safety pin.

To Perform
Lay the string across the table so the ends are to the right and left. Open the handkerchief and place it over the center of the string. It's important that both ends of the string stick out from under the handkerchief (photo 1).

Ask if someone can lend you a finger ring—any type will do. Now bring out the little safety pin and drop it on the table.

Pick up the ring and safety pin, then slide your hands under the handkerchief. Put down the safety pin so you hold only the ring.

Take the center of the string and pull it through the ring making a small loop (photo 2, in which the handkerchief has been removed so you can see what's happening under it).

Next, pick up the safety pin and open it. Stick the safety pin through the two strings (the point of the pin must pierce the center of each strand of string) to the right of the loop you've just made (photo 3, in which the handkerchief has been removed so you can see what's happening under it). It may take some practice because you cannot see what your hands are doing and you do not want to stick yourself with the pin!

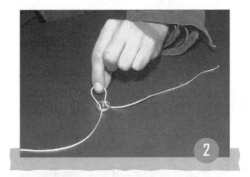

Once the pin is in place, stick your left first finger into the loop of string you pulled out a moment earlier and press it firmly against the table (photo 4, in which the handkerchief has been removed so you can see what's happening under it).

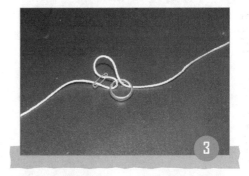

Ask someone to pull the right end of the string. Once the string is pulled taut, the safety pin will press against the ring and hold it in place on the string as it emerges from beneath the handkerchief (photo 5 shows the spectator's hand pulling the ring into view). You must keep your left first fin-

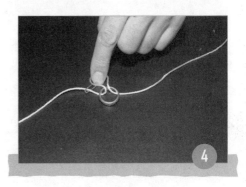

ger in the loop until the string has slipped all the way around it. The audience will not see that the left end of the string disappears under the handkerchief for a few seconds longer than it should.

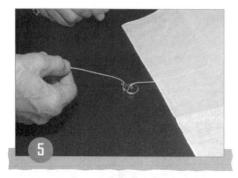

When you feel the end of the string with your left fingers, grab it and pull the handkerchief away with your right hand so the audience can see that the ring has magically become linked to the string. Remove the safety pin and hold the string up for everyone to see (photo 6).

Finally, return the ring to the person from whom you borrowed it.

11. ━

TWO-CARD MONTE

Criss shows two cards, the jack of hearts and the six of clubs. He puts the jack of hearts behind his back and asks someone which card he has placed out of sight. The person will say, "jack of hearts." Criss magically removes the six of clubs from behind his back.

To Prepare

Two special cards are needed: one has two faces, the six of clubs on one side and the jack of hearts on the other (it is called a double-faced card). The other card has a back on both sides (it is called a double-backed card). You'll need four regular playing cards to make these. Simply glue a six of clubs and a jack of hearts together back-to-back. Put them under a stack of books to dry. Then glue any two cards together face-to-face and put them under some books as well. Once the cards are dry you're ready.

You also need one normal six of clubs and one normal jack of hearts. Place the normal six of clubs in your right rear pants pocket, the face of the card toward you. Place the normal jack of hearts in the left breast pocket of your shirt, face toward you.

To Perform

Bring out the two fake cards, holding them in your right hand. The double-backed card is on top of the double-faced card and spread to the right (photo 1). The audience sees one facedown card and a faceup six of clubs. Your right thumb presses lightly on top of the facedown

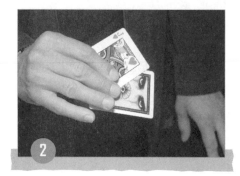

card while your right fingers press upward against the underside of the double-faced card.

Now you're going to display both sides of the cards. This requires a secret move that's easy to learn. You must do two simple things at the same time. First, turn your right hand over until it is palm down. Second, your thumb and fingers slide the two cards in opposite directions—your thumb slides the facedown card away from you, while your fingers slide the faceup card toward you (photo 2). Both of these simple things must be done simultaneously, so that your thumb and fingers are exchanging the positions of the cards *as your hand turns over.*

To those watching it looks like you're displaying two regular cards—each with a normal face on one side and a back on the other.

Turn your right hand palm up again, reversing the secret move so the faceup six of clubs is spread to the left beneath the facedown card.

Your left hand takes the facedown card and inserts it into your left shirt pocket so it goes between the card already in your pocket and your chest.

Your right hand, holding the six of clubs, goes behind your back. Ask a person to name the card that's behind your back. The person will say "six of clubs." Secretly flip the card over with your right fingers and bring the card back around in front of you to reveal the jack of hearts. Your left hand removes the double-backed card from your left shirt pocket and returns it to your right hand so it is on top of the faceup jack and spread to the right.

Turn your right hand palm down, performing the secret move to show the six of clubs as the card just removed from your pocket. Turn your right hand palm up again, reversing the secret move. The jack of hearts and a facedown card will now be visible.

Your left hand takes the facedown card and inserts it into your left shirt pocket so it goes between the card already in your pocket and your chest.

Your right hand, holding the jack of hearts, goes behind your back. Ask a person to name the card that's behind your back. The person will say "jack of hearts." Say, *"No, I have the jack of hearts here,"* as your left hand removes the normal card (outermost) from your left shirt pocket. At the moment that your left hand turns the card around so the face of the jack of hearts is revealed everyone will be watching your left hand. So, your right hand inserts the double-faced card into your rear pants pocket and removes the normal six of clubs.

Now your right hand can bring the six of clubs out from behind your back. Toss both cards onto the table for examination.

12.

SPOON BENDING FOR BEGINNERS

Criss lets someone hand him an ordinary metal spoon from the table. He takes it and, with great effort, bends it completely in half. A second later he magically restores it to its original state.

To Prepare

You need to be sitting at a table that has some silverware on it. You can use either a fork or spoon for this trick.

To Perform

Ask someone to hand you any spoon or fork on the table. Take whichever you're given—say it's the spoon—and make a fist around the handle with your right hand so the bowl sticks out the bottom. The back of the spoon's bowl, the rounded part, should be touching the table (photo 1).

Curl your left fingers around the top of the spoon's handle (photo 2). You should be holding the spoon high enough so that the top of the handle is inside your fist and cannot be seen. To make it look like you're bending the spoon, press firmly downward with both hands. Let the spoon's handle slip out the back of your fist and move downward so that the bowl of the spoon bends flatly on the table (photo 3 is what the audience sees, photo 4 is an exposed view). The people cannot see that you are not still holding the handle upright, so it looks like the spoon is bent.

Open your hands flatly over the spoon, covering it. Act as if you're exerting great strength as you cause the spoon to mysteriously straighten out to its original form, then lift both hands to reveal it.

Advanced Version:

You can add a nifty touch to this by having a nickel hidden in your left hand before you take the spoon. When you get into position, push the nickel up to the top of your fist with your left thumb (photo 5, photo 6 is a close-up)—the nickel appears to be the upper end of the spoon's handle! Perform the trick exactly as explained and, after the spoon has apparently been bent, the people can still see what appears to

be the handle of the spoon protruding from the top of your fist. As you turn both hands palm down over the spoon, your right thumb slides

the nickel under your right hand so it is no longer visible. After you pull your hands back so the people can see the straightened spoon on the table, casually put your hands in your pockets. While there, your right hand drops the nickel.

13.

METAL BEND VANISH

Criss takes a spoon between his hands, magically bends it, then twists it into nothingness.

To Prepare

You must be sitting at a table opposite everyone watching in order to perform this trick. The perfect moment to do this is immediately after the end of "Spoon Bending for Beginners."

To Perform

Hold the spoon suspended horizontally between the palms of your hands, near the table edge (photo 1).

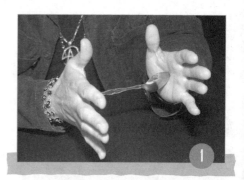

Bring the fingertips of both hands together (photo 2). At the same time, move your hands toward you until they are just past the table edge (photo 3). Note that the bottoms of your hands

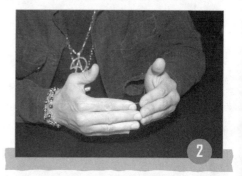

actually rest on the table. Secretly let the spoon fall into your lap (photo 4).

Now, lift your hands about a foot and move them forward, but hold them the same way so the audience thinks the spoon is still behind them (photo 5).

Say, *"The spoon looks solid, but it's really soft."* Move your hands as if you are bending the spoon (photo 6). Then continue, *"In fact, if you're not careful, it can turn into nothing."* As you say, "nothing," make a crumpling motion with the fingers of both hands, then open them to reveal that the spoon has disappeared (photo 7).

14. 〜

BLOW-OUT!

Criss drapes a paper napkin over his left hand and borrows a coin from someone. After he puts the coin in the middle of the napkin, he crushes it into a ball and puts it under that person's hand. Criss magically produces the borrowed coin by blowing it out of a plastic straw before opening the napkin and revealing that there's nothing in it.

To Prepare

You need an unwrapped plastic straw, a paper napkin, and a coin.

To Perform

Borrow a coin from someone and ask the person to mark it with a pen by writing his name or initials—you'll need a permanent marker for this, something like a Sharpie.

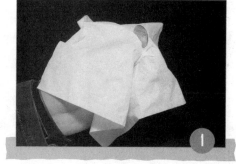

At the same time, turn your left hand palm up. Bring your left thumb and fingers together as if you're holding something (even though you're not), then lay the tissue over them.

Take the marked coin with your right hand. Place the coin into your left hand so your left thumb and fingers can grasp it through the tissue (photo 1). Without pausing, using your right fingers push the coin firmly downward—it secretly breaks through the bottom of the tissue

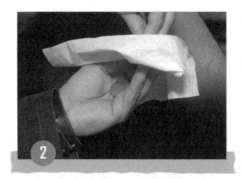

and drops into your left hand (photo 2). To everyone watching it appears as if you have just placed the coin insided the tissue.

Your right hand squeezes the tissue into a small ball and hands it to the person who marked the coin (photo 3). Ask him to hold the tissue tightly in his closed fist. When your right hand takes the tissue away from your left hand, your must turn your left hand over, keeping your fingers *slightly* curled—but not too much!—so the coin hidden in your hand is not seen by the people watching.

Pick up the straw with your right hand and gently tap the back of the person's hand, which is covering the napkin. Ask him if he felt anything. He will say "no."

Put one end of the straw in your mouth. Grab the bottom of the straw with your left hand, making a fist around it. Blow into the straw and let the coin drop out of your left hand at the same time (photo 4). It appears as if you've blown the coin through the straw.

Take the napkin from under the person's hand and rip it into little pieces as you open it. You must tear the napkin up so the person does not find the little hole you made when you pushed the coin through it earlier.

15. —

HOW TO
VANISH A COIN:
THE FRENCH DROP

To Prepare

You will need an ordinary quarter.

One of the basic things a magician must know is how to make a coin disappear. Even though it's not that difficult, you'll have to practice a bit and follow these in-
structions closely.

To Perform

First, take a quarter and hold
it in your left hand exactly as you
see in photo 1: your left hand is
palm up, the fingers are pointing to the right. The coin is held
by its edge between your thumb
and first finger.

Hold your right hand with its
palm toward you and your fingers pointing to the left (photo 2).
Your hands should be held at a
comfortable height, a few inches

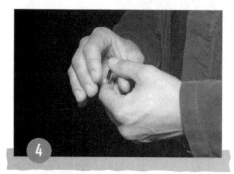

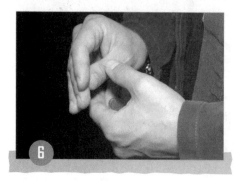

above waist level if you're standing. If you're sitting, then they have to be above the tabletop.

Bring your right hand over to your left hand—your right hand is apparently going to take the coin. Your right fingers move in front of the coin, covering it from the audience, while your thumb goes behind the coin (photo 3 is what the audience sees, photo 4 is an exposed view).

The minute the audience can no longer see the coin, raise your left thumb *very* slightly—just enough to allow the coin to fall inward onto your left fingers (photo 5).

Press your right thumb against the inner side of your right fingers, exactly as if you are holding the coin in place (but of course you're not, since it has fallen onto your left fingers—but you must mimic what you are supposed to be doing) (photo 6).

Several things now happen at the same time: raise your right hand, turning it palm up so your fingers point upward (photo 7).

Watch your right hand intently (photo 8). If you watch your right hand, so will the audience. As you are watching your right hand ascend, your left hand drops away and curls into a *loose* fist.

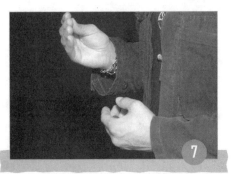

Lean forward and blow on your right fingers. Rub your thumb and fingertips together, then turn your hand toward the audience and open it to show that the coin has vanished (photo 9).

If you have a pen in the left breast pocket, you can secretly get rid of the coin in the following way. After you've supposedly taken the coin in your right hand, your left hand goes to your left breast pocket. Dip your fingers inside and drop the coin, then remove the pen. Wave the pen over your closed right fist, then open your hand to reveal that the coin has vanished!

Advanced Blow-Out:

Now that you know how to properly vanish a coin, we can do the trick "Blow-Out" a bit differently. Have a straw (already out of its paper wrapper) lying on the table in front of you.

Borrow a quarter from someone and pretend to take it with your right hand as just explained. While your right hand moves upward, pretending to hold the coin, your left hand moves downward and picks up the straw from the table (photo 10). You can do this even though the coin is resting inside your left fingers, and holding the straw gives your left hand a natural "look."

Instead of vanishing the coin, your right hand pretends to put it in your mouth. Now perform the last part of "Blow-Out" exactly as explained: your left hand raises the straw to your mouth. Once your right hand grasps the top part of the straw, your left hand can make a fist around the bottom. Blow through the straw and allow the quarter to drop to the table, falling out of your left hand. It looks as if you've blown the quarter through the straw.

16 . ~

COIN FROM ROLL

Criss breaks open a dinner roll and finds a coin inside.

To Prepare

You should be sitting at the dinner table, either at someone's home or in a restaurant where you find dinner rolls on the table. A quarter is resting on the tips of your right fingers (photo 1) while your fingers are curled in a loose fist.

To Perform

Ask someone at the table to please pass you a roll. The person will hand you the basket of rolls—take it with your left hand and place it on the table. Look at the various rolls as if they're somehow different from one another, then pick up any roll with your left hand.

Bring your right hand up to meet your left hand and put the roll onto your right fingers directly over the coin (photo 2).

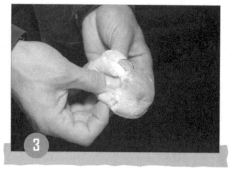

Act as if the roll is a little heavy and say, *"That's odd."* Break open the top of the roll with both thumbs, at the same time pushing the coin up into the roll from beneath with your fingers (photo 3). The people will see a coin inside the roll!

Let someone take the coin out.

Break the roll completely in half and place it on your bread plate. By breaking it in half, you destroy the evidence.

Advanced Version: If you have learned "How to Vanish a Coin," you can combine it with "Coin from Roll" to produce an even better trick.

First, borrow a quarter from someone and have that person put his or her initials on it with a permanent marker, like a Sharpie.

Next, vanish the coin exactly as explained: afterward the coin will be resting inside your left hand, on your fingers (the left hand is closed in a loose fist). Ask another person to pick up one of the dinner rolls and hand it to you—take it with your *right* hand. Place the roll over the coin on your left fingers. Break the roll open as already explained, secretly pushing the coin up from beneath to produce the coin from inside.

17. ⌒

OOPS!

Criss accidentally drops a coin on the floor. He picks it up and makes it disappear.

To Prepare
You need a coin.

To Perform
You can either borrow the coin or simply bring it out of your pocket. Talk for a moment and, in the process, "accidentally" drop the coin on the floor.

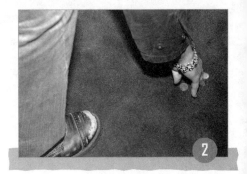

It's best if the coin falls about twelve inches in front of one of your feet (photo 1). If it falls too far away, walk over to it. Position yourself so that the coin is between you and anyone who's watching.

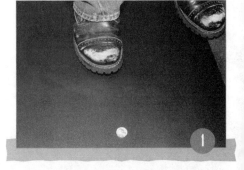

Bend over *as if* to pick up the coin and rest your fingertips on the ground directly in front of it (photo 2). Instead of actually lifting it, snap your fingers in the direction of your foot, secretly sliding the coin

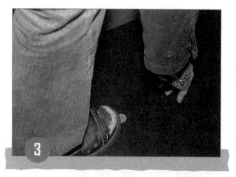

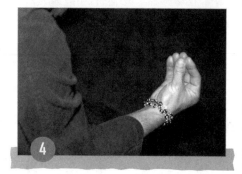

under your shoe (photo 3 shows the tail end of the coin's journey just before it slides out of sight under the shoe).

Immediately raise your hand as if you're holding the coin, fingers and thumb pressed together, and stand up (photo 4).

Place the nonexistent coin in your left hand, which closes into a fist. Snap your right fingers, then slowly open your left hand to reveal that the coin has vanished. (Make sure to show your right hand empty, too.)

18. ~

KNIFED!

Criss places a knife under a napkin and it disappears.

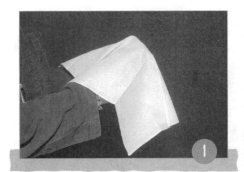

To Prepare
You need a table knife and a napkin or handkerchief. You must be wearing either a long-sleeved shirt with the sleeves rolled down or a jacket.

To Perform
Unfold the napkin and drape it over your left hand (photo 1). Your right hand takes the knife (photo 2) and puts it under the napkin. Secretly insert the knife, handle first, all the way into your left sleeve (photo 3 is an x-ray view: you can see through the napkin).

While it's still hidden under the napkin, quickly close your right hand into a fist and stick

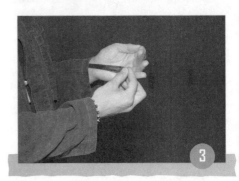

233

your right first finger up in the air (photo 4 is an x-ray view).

Your left thumb and fingers grasp the napkin at the very tip of your right first finger (photo 5). As your left hand lifts the napkin, curl your right first finger. When the napkin clears your empty right hand, it will appear as if the knife is under the napkin (held at its tip by your left hand). Toss the napkin up in the air, catching it when it comes down again. Display both sides to prove that the knife has vanished.

19.

SUGAR COIN

Criss shows a quarter and lets a person look at it and remember its date. He makes the quarter disappear, then reaches into the little basket of sugar packets that has been on the table all along and removes one. He tears it open to reveal the quarter inside. He gives it to the person who verifies that it has the same date.

To Prepare

You need two quarters with the same date and a sugar packet. You want to perform this trick when you're in a restaurant where there are normally small bowls filled with sugar packets.

Take one of the sugar packets when no one is looking, then head off to the restroom for a moment. Secretly make a little slit in the upper edge of the sugar packet (photo 1). The slit should be just big enough so that you can slide one of the quarters completely inside (photo 2). When you return to your seat, secretly drop this prepared sugar

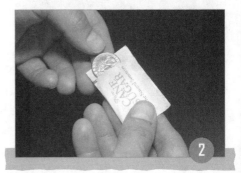

packet into the dish with the other sugar packets as you move it out of the way. Make sure you remember the position of the packet you've just loaded into the bowl. (Don't forget to check out the Advanced Version of this trick.)

To Perform

Show the other quarter, the one with the identical date to the quarter you've secretly loaded into the sugar packet, to the audience and ask one person to read the date aloud so everyone knows it.

Criss has already explained "How to Vanish a Coin: The French Drop," but if you haven't read that yet, please go back and do it now. You'll need to have already practiced and learned that sleight in order to perform this trick.

Hold the quarter in your left hand, in proper position for the vanish. Pretend to take the coin with your right hand, secretly allowing it to fall onto your left fingers.

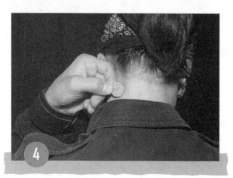

Pick your left arm up so your right hand can pretend to rub the coin into your left elbow (photo 3). You will find that your left hand automatically moves near the collar of your shirt—it's easy to drop the concealed coin down your collar (photo 4). It will fall into your shirt, but the audience won't see that—they will be watching your right hand rub the coin they think it holds into your left elbow.

Open your right hand and move it away from your elbow to show that the coin has disappeared. Show both hands to be completely empty.

Reach over to the sugar bowl and take out the sugar packet you have prepared in advance. Hold it by the left long edge with your left thumb and fingers. The side with the slit should be toward you so the audience cannot see it (photo 5). Your right thumb and fingers rip open the top of the packet by tearing along the secret slit (photo 6). This cleverly destroys the evidence!

Turn the sugar packet upside down so all the sugar and the quarter fall out (photo 7). Ask someone to pluck the coin out of the sugar and read the date.

Advanced Version: You can make the trick more mystifying by doing some of the prep work in advance. Use a packet of Sweet'n Low—you know that every restaurant will have these in their sugar bowl. Make an X on one of your quarters with a marker. Next, slit open the packet of Sweet'n Low very carefully and put your marked quarter inside. Now glue the packet closed. You'll find that it's much easier to secretly load the packet of Sweet'n Low into the sugar bowl at the restaurant if you have it all prepared and in your pocket in advance—you have much more time, and many more opportunities to innocently push the sugar bowl out of the way during the meal. When you want to perform the trick, bring out the other quarter with a matching date and openly draw an almost identical X on it with the marker. Now proceed as already explained.

20. ~

TAPPED OUT!

Criss is holding a coin in his left hand and a pen in his right. He tells the audience that he will make the coin disappear by tapping it with the pen. However, the pen disappears instead. Criss shows the audience that he secretly stuck the pen behind his ear when they weren't looking. Then, the coin vanishes.

To Prepare

You need a pen and a coin. You must be standing when you perform this trick.

To Perform

Stand so your left side is facing the person for whom you are doing the trick. The coin is lying on your palm-up left hand, while your right hand holds the pen by its lower end (photo 1).

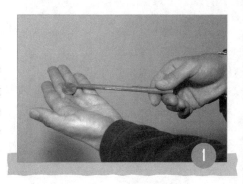

Tell the person that you will make the coin vanish on the count of "three." Tap the coin with the pen twice (counting aloud *"one," "two"*), each time raising your right hand very high so the pen is near your right ear. On *"three,"* your right hand swings up and actually sticks the pen behind your ear (photo 2; photo 3 is a close-up in which

you can see how Criss sticks the pen under the headgear he's wearing; if you're not wearing anything on your head, then just slip it behind your ear).

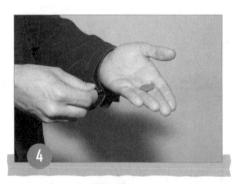

Don't pause—immediately lower your right hand as if to tap the coin a third time (photo 4). Look at your right hand with surprise when you see that the pen has disappeared.

Tell the person that you will let him know the secret if he promises never to tell anyone else. He will say yes.

Turn around so your right side is now facing him. Show him that the pen is behind your ear (photo 5). At the same time, as your right hand is pointing to the pen and pulling it out from behind your ear, your left hand secretly drops the coin into your left pocket. Try not to move your left arm too much when you do this.

Your right hand takes the pen as you turn so your left side is again facing the person. The funny thing is, the person will not yet notice that the coin isn't in your left hand.

Begin to tap the pen on the coin (photo 6). Act surprised that the coin has now disappeared! Apologize to the person for all the confusion and let him keep the pen as a souvenir.

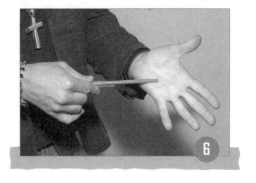

21. ⟶

KICKED!

Criss shuffles a deck of cards, then allows someone to select a card, remember it, and replace it in the center of the deck. It is apparently lost. Criss places the deck on the floor and gently kicks it with his foot. The deck magically cuts itself at the person's card.

To Prepare

You need a deck of cards and a pinch of salt.

If you're sitting at a table, have a little pile of salt on the table (you really only need a few grains). If you are standing, have some salt in one of your right side pockets.

To Perform

Give the deck of cards to a person for shuffling. Afterward, take the cards back and hold them in your left hand, facedown. Ask the person to cut off any amount of cards as you point to the table indicating to your helper where to put the upper half she cuts off.

Ask your helper to look at the card on top of the left-hand pile. While she is looking at the card, press the first finger of your right hand into the little pile of salt that's either on the table or in your right pocket. Do *not* wet your finger before you do this—a few grains of salt will stick to it without any help (photo 1 is an exposed view).

Say, "*Have you remembered your card? Good. Now please put it back.*" The person will return her card on top of the pile in your left hand. Now, point to the top of that pile of cards in your left hand with your right first finger and lightly touch it (photo 2). You will secretly leave a few grains of salt there as you say, "*Please pick up the cards from the table and put them on top.*" Once the person has placed the cards on top of those in your left hand, the deck will have been completely reassembled—with a little something extra on top of the chosen card.

Gently place the deck of cards on the floor. Give the cards a little nudge with your foot. Because you have secretly placed some salt on top of the person's card, the deck will cut itself at that point (photo 3—the chosen card is the one whose back is most visible in the center of the spread). Lift off the top card of the lower half and turn it over to reveal the chosen card.

243

22. ⟶

FLATLINE

Criss tells his friends that even though he looks okay, he actually died performing in the TV series MINDFREAK. He proves it by asking some of them to take his pulse—but he doesn't have one and so he must be dead.

To Prepare

You need a small round ball, about the size of a golf ball. Place it under your armpit—actually against your skin.

To Perform

This can be a great mystery, but you have to present it properly. You don't just walk up to someone and ask him or her to take your pulse— you have to set it up so they get creeped out. A good story might be that you're already dead, and you can prove it because you have no pulse.

Another way to present it might be to say, *"I went to see a great zombie movie last night, and it scared me so much that every time I think about it my heart stops beating."* Ask someone to feel your pulse. He does this by putting his first two fingers on your wrist. Say, *"Do you feel my pulse? Good. Now I'm going to think about that zombie movie—you'll feel my pulse vanish as my heart stops beating."* Slowly squeeze your arm against your body so the ball in your armpit puts pressure against your skin. As you do that, your pulse will become faint and stop. Don't stay that way too long—release the pressure after about ten seconds and allow the person to feel your pulse again.

23 . ➤

FLOATING CUP

Criss waves his hands over an empty cup and it mysteriously begins to float.

To Prepare
You need a Styrofoam cup.

To Perform
Explain that you're going to exert a magical force over the cup, but don't say what you're going to do. Begin by displaying the cup (photo 1). Grasp the cup, mouth upward, between both hands and bring its bottom down firmly onto the table so it makes a noise (photo 2). At that instant, your left thumb punches its way into the rear of the cup (photo 3)—the sound of this is covered by the sound of the cup hitting the table.

Slowly lift your hands and open them, moving your left thumb slightly (photo 4). Now spread your fingers and the cup will appear to be floating between your hands (photo 5). Once you reach this po-

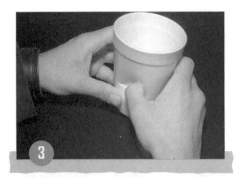

sition, you can slowly and mysteriously move your hands as if the cup is floating and your hands are simply following it. In reality, of course, your left thumb is supporting the cup!

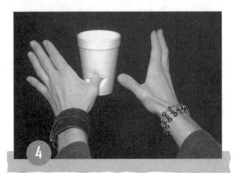

After the cup floats a bit, lower your hands so the cup appears to float down to the table. Then bring your hands together and crush the cup between them (photo 6), breaking it into pieces so no one can examine it and discover the hole in the back.

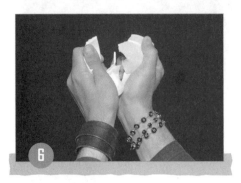

24. ➾

INTO THE MIND

Criss asks someone to think of any number between one and one thousand and write it down on a small Post-it while he has his back turned. Then Criss asks the person to hand the paper to him behind his back. Criss faces forward and reads the person's mind, naming the thought-of number.

To Prepare

You need a Post-it notepad and a pen. You can only perform this bit of mind reading when you are standing close to a wall. It should be about a foot behind you.

To Perform

Begin by handing both the notepad and the pen to someone and say, *"Please think of any number between one and one thousand. Then turn your back and write it down on that notepad. I'll turn my back."*

Suit action to words and turn your back to the spectator so you're facing the wall.

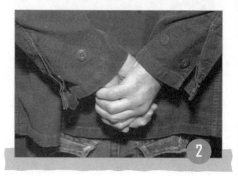

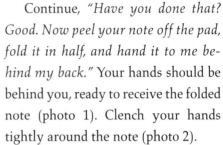

Continue, *"Have you done that? Good. Now peel your note off the pad, fold it in half, and hand it to me behind my back."* Your hands should be behind you, ready to receive the folded note (photo 1). Clench your hands tightly around the note (photo 2).

Now turn around and face the person. Begin to talk about the impossibility of being able to determine which number he or she has chosen. At the same time, stick the note onto the wall behind you (photo 3) and unfold it (photo 4). Clench your now-empty hands behind you in exactly the same position they were in before.

Turn around and face the wall, your back once again toward the person. Say, *"It helps me to concentrate if I can't see your face—watch my hands and concentrate on the number."* You'll find that you can now simply look down and see the number on the open piece of paper stuck to the wall (photo 5).

Close your eyes and begin saying different digits aloud, *"I'm getting closer to your number."* Turn around and face the spectator. Announce the number he or she wrote down. At the same time, your hands pull the Post-it off the wall and fold it in half. Bring your hands around in front of you and hand the note back to the spectator.

Four Tricks with a Key Card

The use of what magicians call a *key card* allows you to locate chosen cards very easily.

Put any card that you can easily remember, such as the ace of spades, on the bottom of the deck. (Or you can simply glance at whatever card happens to be on the bottom of the deck and remember it.)

Now place the deck facedown on the table. Say, *"Please cut off about half of the deck—it doesn't have to be exact, of course, just don't cut off a little packet."* Wait until the person does as you ask and cuts off a part of the deck, then say, *"Please put the packet you just cut off on the table next to the rest of the deck."*

Continue, *"Now, look at the top card of the original packet—the card you cut to."* If the spectator doesn't quite understand, you can always indicate what you want the person to do with your hands, but don't touch the cards yet.

"Please put the card back on top of the packet you cut off." Once that's been done, say, *"Now complete the cut—in other words, pick up the bottom of the deck and put it on top of your card, burying it."* That's it: follow those instructions and the card you are remembering will be directly on top of the card the person cut to.

The trick, of course, is what to do from here. Here are three ways to produce a miracle.

25.

CARD THOUGHT

Turn the deck faceup and spread it across the table. Glance at the cards, looking for the card you're remembering. When you spot it, look at the card directly to the right—that is the chosen card (photo 1, in which the card you are remembering, your key card, is the ace of spades; the chosen card in this example is the three of clubs—it could be any card when you actually perform the trick).

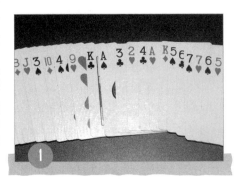

Remember the chosen card. When you do this, do *not* stare intently at the deck for too long. Now square up the cards, then gaze into the spectator's eyes and slowly, *slowly* act as if you are reading her mind, *"I can see the card . . . it's a . . . wait . . . a six . . . no . . . perhaps the three . . . YES,* the three of . . . I see red, so it must be the . . . no . . . definitely black . . . the three of clubs. You chose the three of clubs."* Of course you would name the card you see next to your key card—we're only using the three of clubs as an example.

26. ⟶

HELLTROMISM/
MUSCLE READING

With the cards still spread faceup on the table, you have glanced down and ascertained both the identity and location of the chosen card. Hold out your hand, palm down, with the first finger extended. Ask the person who chose the card to gently hold your wrist (photo 2). Guide your hand above the cards on the table from side to side and all over the cards, your finger pointing downward like a dowsing rod. Eventually, after several false dips downward, bring your finger directly down onto the chosen card.

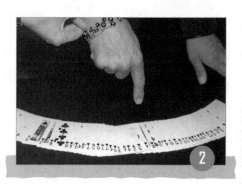

27 . ⟶

CARD STAB

With the cards still spread faceup on the table, you have glanced down and ascertained both the identity and location of the chosen card. Now, using both hands, smush the cards around into a messed-up pile, always keeping your eye on the chosen card.

Now pick up a butter knife and hold it, point down, in your right hand. (Note that you must *not* do this on a surface that's fragile, like glass, or valuable, like a nice wooden table. You should put a wooden tray or newspaper under the cards before you start.) Ask the person who chose the card to grasp your right wrist, then hold the knife poised about two feet above the cards.

Quickly bring your right hand straight down and stab the chosen card (photo 3). Lift the knife straight up—the card will come with it and you can flash the bottom so everyone sees the knife really goes through it (photo 4).

28. ⚊

THE NEXT CARD I TURN OVER WILL BE YOURS

After the spectator cuts the deck, remembers a card, and loses it in the deck, Criss is able to find it in an unexpected way.

To Prepare

This effect also relies upon the use of a key card. Let's assume that, for our example, we are again going to use the ace of spades. Make sure it's on the bottom of the deck.

To Perform

The same procedure for the preceding three tricks is used to control the key card to be above the chosen card. Place the deck facedown on the table. Say, *"Please cut off about half of the deck—it doesn't have to be exact, of course, just don't cut off a little packet."* Wait until the person does as you ask and cuts off a part of the deck, then say, *"Please put the packet you just cut off on the table next to the rest of the deck."*

Continue, *"Now, look at the top card of the original packet—the card you cut to."* If the spectator doesn't quite understand, you can always indicate with your hands what you want the person to do, but don't touch the cards yet.

"Please put the card back on top of the packet you cut off." Once that's been done, say, *"Now complete the cut—in other words, pick up*

the bottom of the deck and put it on top of your card, burying it." The ace of spades, your key card, will be directly on top of the card the person cut to.

Place the facedown deck into dealing position in your left hand. Begin dealing the cards to the table one at a time, turning each one faceup as you do. Do not deal them into a neat pile—make a sloppy pile so the ends of the cards are sticking out all over the place.

While you are dealing, watch for your key card. When you turn the ace of spades faceup, you know that the *very next card* is going to be the chosen card. However, don't pause or hesitate, just continue dealing and remember the identity of the chosen card when you see it. Also, make sure the end of it sticks out from the pile on the table so it remains in view.

After you've dealt another four or five cards faceup onto the pile, say, *"The next card I turn over will be yours."* Of course, the person will immediately assume you've made a mistake because you've already turned the chosen card faceup.

However, you do *not* turn over the next card on the deck. Rather, your right hand immediately goes directly to the chosen card on the table, pulls it out of the spread, and turns it facedown.

Not only does this get a chuckle because of the gag, but it's also pretty damn mysterious, too.

29 . ⌒

QUARTER THROUGH TABLE

Criss removes a coin from his pocket and places it on the table. He picks it up, moves it to a different spot, and then pushes it through the table.

To Prepare

You'll need two identical coins. One should be lying on the table, the other is in your lap. There must be a napkin and a knife on the table. During the course of your meal, or whatever other tricks you're doing, casually give the napkin an upward fold in the center of one side—so it's very slightly tented. The napkin should be in front of you, just slightly right of center, with the tented side facing to the *left* (photo 1).

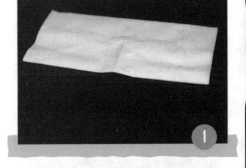

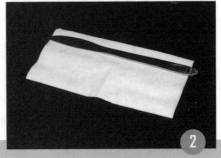

Now place a table knife (or fork, or whatever) on the right side of the napkin to anchor it in place (photo 2).

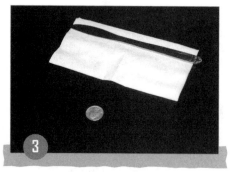

To Perform

Position the coin on the table so it's about two inches to the left of the tented napkin (photo 3). Lower your palm-down right hand over the coin and, with your right thumb, flick the coin to the right, under the napkin (photos 4 and 5). This is done secretly! Your thumb knocks the coin to the right the instant it's covered by your hand. This will take some practice because you don't want to hit the coin either too lightly or too strongly. It must slide rapidly under the napkin—that's why you tented it—and stop. If you tap the coin too hard, it'll hit the knife and clink.

Without pausing, pretend that you are picking up the coin with your right hand, holding it between the thumb and fingertips of the palm-down hand (photo 6).

While your right hand is busy, your left hand has picked up the duplicate coin from your lap and is holding it with its edge pressed against the underside of the table (photo 7 is an exposed view from beneath—the people watching cannot see this). Your left hand should be directly below your right hand (separated by the table, of course).

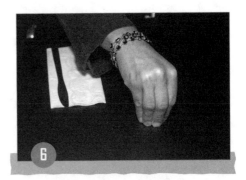

Your right hand presses down on the table and moves around a bit as you say, *"I'm looking for the soft spot."* As your right hand moves, your left hand moves directly below, keeping the coin's edge in contact with the underside of the table, and the scraping sound that results sounds as if it's coming from the coin in your right hand.

After moving the coin around a bit, pick a spot, then pretend to push it through the table with your right hand, pressing down with only your second finger and spreading all the other fingers so the people can see that the coin is no longer there (photo 8). At the exact same moment, your left fingers push the coin they're holding up against the table with a loud *snap*—the lower edge flicks off your thumb and hits the underside of the table to produce the noise (photo 9).

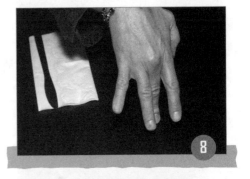

Raise your right hand and show it's completely empty. Your left hand brings the coin out from beneath the table to conclude.

Advanced Version: Have a penny, nickel, dime, and quarter in your lap. This way you can ask someone to hand you any coin—it doesn't matter. No matter what coin it is, you'll have a duplicate in your lap.

30.

DÉJÀ VU

Criss opens a matchbook and pulls out a single match. He strikes it, lets it burn, then blows it out and makes it disappear. The burnt match reappears inside the matchbook!

To Prepare

You need an ordinary matchbook that you must prepare in advance. Remove a few matches from different spots in the front row. Bend one match, near the center, forward—so it's away from the other matches but still attached at the bottom. Being very careful, ignite one of the matches you just tore out and use it to burn the protruding match (photo 1). Do not allow any of the other matches to ignite— just the one you've bent forward and then blow it out.

After the match cools *completely,* fold it back inside the matchbook beside the other matches. Now close the matchbook.

To Perform

Bring out the matchbook and open it so the matches face you and can't be seen by anyone yet. Using your right thumb and first finger,

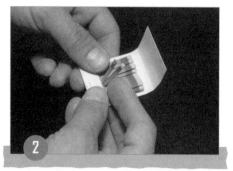

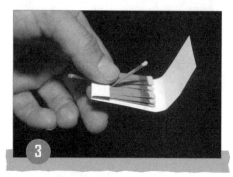

bend two matches away from the book: the burnt one and the one beside it (photo 2). Press the burnt one all the way down so it's flat and under your left thumb (photo 3 is an exposed view—Criss has raised his left thumb a bit so you can see the match beneath it). Then lower your hands so the audience can see the matches, and with your right hand tear off the other match you've bent downward (photo 4).

Strike the torn-off match and allow it to burn for a second, then blow it out. Wait for it to cool, then place it on the table in front of you—about three inches forward of the edge.

Your right hand returns to assist in closing the matchbook. At the same time, your left hand tilts the inside of the matchbook toward you (as it was originally) so the matches are no longer visible to anyone watching. As your right hand closes the book, your left thumb levers the burnt match back inside (photo 5). Close the matchbook and place it on the table. Ask a person to place his or her hand over the book, completely covering it.

Now you must make the match that's on the table disappear. You'll do this by using something magicians call *lapping*. Turn your right hand palm down, fingers straight, and lower it directly onto the match (photo 6). Draw your hand toward you, sliding it inward until it leaves the table (photo 7)—the match, hidden beneath your fingers, will fall into your lap. Move your right thumb under your fingers as if it's holding the match in place (photo 8).

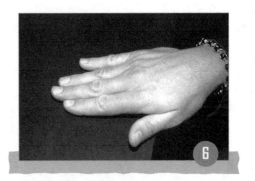

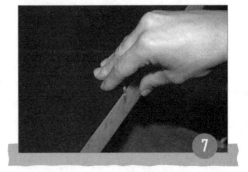

Raise your right hand to your mouth and blow on your fingers, then make a tossing motion toward the matchbook under the person's hand. Show your right hand empty. Ask that person to lift his or her hand and open the matchbook to reveal that the match has returned.

31. ⬤—

SNEAKY SHEEP

Criss places five coins on the table and refers to them as sheep. Then he displays two more coins, one in each hand, and says these are two thieves who've come to steal the sheep. He picks up three sheep with his right hand and two sheep with his left, and yet when he opens the left hand, it only contains the two thieves, while all five sheep magically appear in his right hand.

To Prepare

You'll need seven identical coins—quarters are best to use because they're the largest coins and can be easily handled.

To Perform

Bring out your coins (or borrow them if possible) and arrange them in two horizontal rows on the table (photo 1). The outer row contains five coins while the inner row contains two. Say, *"Five little sheep and two nasty thieves."*

Pick up the two coins in the inner row, one in your right hand and the other in your left, and make a fist around each as you say, *"The nasty thieves hide behind the bushes until no one is looking."*

Continue, *"Now that no one's around, the thieves sneak out and steal the sheep."* During the following sequence, you must keep your hands closed loosely into fists so no one can see inside them. Your right hand picks up the first "sheep," using your right thumb to nip it against the side of your finger (photo 2) before drawing it completely inside the fist (photo 3 shows the coin just before it goes completely inside your hand).

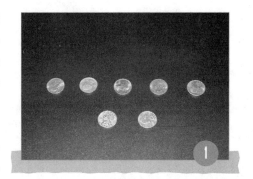

Your left hand picks up the second "sheep" the same way, drawing it into the fist with your left thumb.

Your right hand picks up the third "sheep."

Your left hand picks up the fourth "sheep."

Your right hand picks up the fifth "sheep."

You now have three coins in your left hand and four in your right.

Say, *"The thieves heard a noise and got scared, so they put the sheep back."* First, your left hand puts one of its coins back on the table (let's call it the first coin).

Then, your right hand puts a second coin back on the table.

Your left hand puts a third coin back on the table.

263

Your right hand puts a fourth coin back on the table.

Your left hand puts a fifth coin back on the table.

You now have two coins in your right hand and no coins in your left hand. You are one ahead of the audience: they believe you still have one coin in each hand—it gets better.

Continue, *"After a minute or two went by, the thieves ran out and grabbed the sheep one more time."*

Your right hand picks up the first "sheep."

Your left hand picks up the second "sheep."

Your right hand picks up the third "sheep."

Your left hand picks up the fourth "sheep."

Your right hand picks up the fifth "sheep."

Say, *"Then the thieves went to sleep. When they woke up in the morning they were very disappointed to discover that they were sleeping together,"* open your left hand to reveal only two coins. Conclude, *". . . and all the sheep were safe behind the other bush,"* as you open your right hand to reveal five coins.

32 . ━

ASHES 2 ASHES

*Criss asks a woman to hold her hands palm down in front of her.
He asks the woman to name "right" or "left." He uses the hand she
chooses and asks her to close it into a fist, dropping her other hand
to her side. He reaches into an ashtray and takes a small bit of
cigarette ash on his finger. He waves his hand over hers, crumpling
his fingers, asking her if she felt any heat. She says no. He opens
his hand to reveal that the ashes on his finger have vanished. Criss
tells her to open her hand—when she does, she discovers that the
ashes are now on her palm.*

To Prepare

The only thing you need is
an ashtray with some cigarette
ash in it. It should be nearby—
close enough that you can reach
it. Before the trick begins, secretly lick the tip of your right
second finger and dunk it in the
ash (photo 1). Keep your right
fingers loosely curled so the sto-
len ash isn't seen.

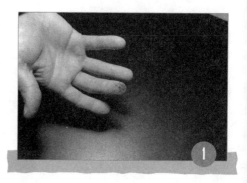

To Perform

Approach a woman and ask her to hold out both hands, palm down.
Reach out and grasp her hands, her right hand with your left, and her

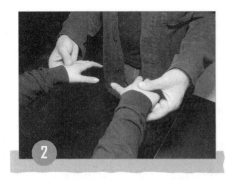

left hand with your right. Grasp them gently between your thumbs, above, and first and second fingertips, on her palms. Move her hands up and down for a moment as if adjusting their height—it is at this moment that you secretly press the ashes onto her left palm with your right second finger (photo 2). Don't forget to press against her right palm as well so everything feels the same to her. Let go of her hands.

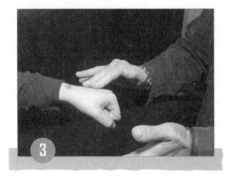

Say, *"Please name right or left on the count of three. One, two, three!"* If she says "left," then ask her to close her left hand into a loose fist and let her right hand drop. If she says "right," ask her to drop her right hand. Then say, *"Please close your left hand into a fist."*

Either way, she ends up with her left hand closed in a fist.

Walk over to where the ashtray is and pick it up with your left hand. Openly touch your right second finger to the ashes, then put the ashtray down. Return to the person and clearly display the ash on your finger.

Touch your finger to the back of her closed fist, putting some ash on it (photo 3). Then vigorously rub your fingers against the back of her hand (you're actually rubbing the ashes away) as you say, *"Do you feel the heat, do you feel it?"*

Hold your hands above and below her hand and concentrate really hard and allow your hands to tremble a bit (photo 4). After a few moments of this, slowly move your right hand away to reveal that the ashes have disappeared from the back of her hand.

Ask the person to turn her hand over and open it to reveal the ashes on her palm (photo 5). She'll scream.

33 . ⟶

NEWSPAPER
PREDICTION

Criss displays a sealed envelope containing a prediction—this is given to someone to hold. Next he picks up a strip cut from a sheet of newspaper and a pair of scissors. He runs the open scissors down the newspaper strip until someone calls stop. He cuts the strip at the point chosen by the spectator. After the top line of the cut-off piece is read aloud, the person holding the envelope rips it open and reads Criss's prediction—they match!

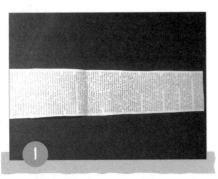

To Prepare

You need a large format newspaper such as the *New York Times* and scissors. Cut a long narrow single column of type from an article that runs the entire length of the page (photo 1). Now cut off the top few lines so the top line of your strip begins in the middle of a sentence (photo 2). You also need a marker, a pad of paper on which to write your prediction, and an envelope in which to seal it.

a screenwriting credit on these recent movies. Don't shed any tears, though. Even without screen credit, top rewrite artists can bank more than $250,000 a week for script revisions and frequently can stay on a movie for months at a

Look at the top line of text and remember it.

One of the most important things to note about this trick is that it cannot be performed for people who are sitting very close to you—you should be at least ten feet away from them.

To Perform

Begin by saying, *"Something amazing is going to happen in a few minutes and I'm going to predict what it is."* Pick up the marker and pad of paper and write the line of type you're remembering from the top of the strip. Afterward, rip the paper off the pad and fold it up. Insert into the envelope, seal it, and hand it to someone to hold.

Now comes the sneaky part: pick up the strip of newspaper and explain that you've cut out a column that has thousands of words on it. However, you hold the strip by the bottom with your left hand so it's upside down! Because you're not too close to the people watching, they can't see it's upside down.

Your right hand picks up the scissors and opens them, moving them around the upper end of the strip of paper (photo 3). Begin to *slowly* move your right hand downward and ask someone to call out stop anywhere he or she likes.

When you are stopped, cut the strip cleanly in two at that point, allowing the bottom portion to fall to the floor.

Place the upper portion of the strip and the scissors out of the way, then pick up the portion of the strip from the floor. When you pick it up, make sure it's right side up as it normally should be.

Hand the strip to someone and ask him or her to read the top line out loud. Once they have, ask the person holding the envelope to rip it open, remove the paper inside, and read the prediction aloud: it will be the same.

34 . ━

TOOTHPICK VANISH

Criss causes a toothpick to vanish and reappear inches from the face of someone watching.

To Prepare

You need a toothpick and a small piece of Scotch tape. Lay the end of the toothpick flatly against the back of your right thumbnail and put the piece of Scotch tape over it (photo 1). Using your left thumb and first finger, twirl the toothpick a few times until you can slide it out from beneath the tape (photo 2)—this leaves a channel in the tape so you can reinsert the toothpick when needed.

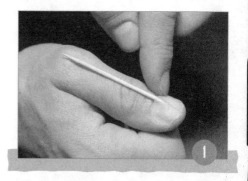

Note that this can only be performed for one person who's standing directly in front of you. Anyone else will see how it's done.

To Perform

Begin with the toothpick hanging from your mouth. Remove it with your left hand. Turn your right hand so your thumb and first finger are up-

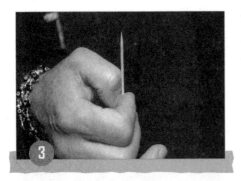

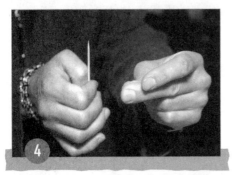

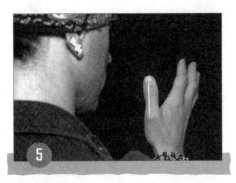

ward. Curl your thumb as much as you can and insert the toothpick into the channel in the tape. Once the toothpick is all the way in, it appears, from the front, that it is being held between your right thumb and first fingertip (photo 3). It's important that you don't let the person watching see you actually insert the toothpick under the tape—in fact, that person should never see the tape at all.

Your left hand, held near your right, snaps its fingers (photo 4). Suddenly move your hands a few inches closer to the person's face—this causes them to lose focus for a second. At the same time, open both your hands, pointing the tip of your right thumb directly toward your face (photo 5 is an exposed view). It will appear to the person watching that the toothpick has vanished. You have to watch your angles, of course, because from the sides anyone can see the toothpick behind your thumb. The person watching will see only your empty hands (photo 6).

To make the toothpick reappear, suddenly retract your hands toward you, at the same time returning your right hand to its original position, apparently holding the toothpick between the tips of the thumb and first finger.

Your right hand places the toothpick back between your lips, which draw it out from beneath the tape as your right hand moves away.

Advanced Version: This can be done without using Scotch tape. Instead of a toothpick, use a match that you've ripped out of a matchbook. Under the guise of a slight cough, bring your right hand up to your mouth and secretly lick the back of your right thumbnail. Leave a nice amount of saliva on it. Now perform the trick exactly as explained but, this time, instead of inserting the end of the toothpick between the Scotch tape and your nail, press the lower end of the match firmly against the saliva. It should stick, allowing you to continue with the presentation. If it doesn't stick, then try using less saliva. Experiment until you figure out exactly the right amount. It would be pretty embarrassing if the match fell off your thumb in the middle of the trick.

35. ⟶

ACES ANYTIME

Criss brings out a deck of cards and hands it to someone with instructions to shuffle it thoroughly. Afterward, he asks the person to feel the interior of the inner breast pocket of his jacket to make certain it's empty, then to place the mixed deck into that pocket. Criss asks the person to name a four of a kind—most people will name aces. Criss inserts his hand into his pocket and, one at a time, mysteriously locates each ace and removes it from his pocket.

To Prepare

You can use any deck of cards. Before you begin, secretly remove the four aces from the deck and insert them into the left breast pocket of your shirt, faces toward you (photo 1). You need to be wearing a jacket with an inside breast pocket.

To Perform

Bring out the deck of cards and shuffle it. Then hand it to someone and ask that person to also shuffle the cards.

Say, *"Would you please put your hand into my pocket and feel that*

it's empty?" Pull open the left side of your jacket and allow the person to stick his or her hand inside your jacket's inner breast pocket. Then, ask the person to drop the deck into that pocket.

Ask, *"Are you a card player? What's your favorite four of a kind?"* Most people will, of course, name the aces because they are the highest cards in the deck and also the most easily recognized. If the person says, "Aces," skip to the next paragraph. If, however, the person names another four of a kind (whatever it is), say, *"Obviously you're not a card player, because the best four of a kind is the four aces. You'll always win with four aces. Let me show you what I can do with my sense of touch."*

Continue, *"Using just the skill of my fingertips, let's see if I can locate the four aces in the deck."* Insert your right hand inside your jacket. Act as if you are inserting your fingers into the jacket pocket containing the deck—but actually insert your thumb into the breast pocket of your shirt (photo 2 is an exposed view—actually your jacket is closed at this point so the audience cannot see what's happening). Pull any one of the aces straight up until it completely clears the pocket (but is still hidden by your jacket), then bring it out into view. The card comes out back toward audience to build tension . . . slowly turn it around to reveal the first ace (photo 3).

Magically locate the remaining three Aces, one at a time, in exactly the same way, by pulling them out of your shirt pocket while the people watching think they're coming out of the deck in your jacket pocket! At the end of the trick, bring the deck of cards out of your pocket (or let someone else remove it) and do another card trick.

36.

PENNY OR DIME?

Criss displays a penny and a dime and places both on the table. He closes one hand into a fist and drops the penny inside. Then he lets someone else drop the dime inside. He asks another person to name either the penny or the dime. The penny is chosen and it vanishes.

To Prepare

You need an ordinary penny and a dime—these can be borrowed from the audience. You must also be sitting at a table opposite everyone.

To Perform

Place the dime and penny on the table about a foot apart and turn both coins over one at a time. Say, *"A dime and a penny."*

Curl your left fingers into a *very loose* fist (photo 1). The opening between your first finger and thumb at the top should go clear down and out the bottom of the hand.

Move your left fist to the edge of the table so that while

the lower side of the hand touches the table edge, the opening at the bottom of the fist is *beyond the edge,* over your lap (photo 2).

Pick up the penny with your right hand and drop it into the top of your fist (photo 3). It will drop straight down, out the bottom, and into your lap (photo 4 shows the penny dropping).

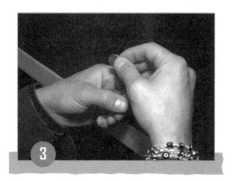

Immediately close your fist a little more tightly and move your left hand forward. Pick up the dime and hand it to someone, asking that person to insert it into your fist.

Say, *"Name either coin, the dime or the penny."* No matter what coin is chosen, the end result is the same: the penny will disappear while the dime remains in your hand. In order to make this logical, you will say one of two things:

*If the penny is named, say, *"Watch,"* snap your fingers, then open your left hand and conclude, *"The coin you chose, the penny, has disappeared. Only the dime is left."*

*If the dime is named, say, *"Watch,"* snap your fingers, then open your left hand and conclude, *"Only the coin you chose, the dime, remains! The penny has vanished."*

Drop the dime on the table to end.

37 . ~

PROPHECY

Criss brings out a deck of cards and hands it to someone with instructions to shuffle it thoroughly. Criss spreads the deck facedown on the table and asks three people to take one card each. Afterward, he gathers the rest of the deck and puts it away.

Next, he takes the three chosen cards and shows them around—it doesn't matter if he sees them. He turns to one person and asks her to remember one of the three cards, but not to say its name aloud. He turns to a different person and asks him to feel the interior of the inner breast pocket of his jacket to make certain it's empty. Then Criss places the three chosen cards into that pocket. Criss looks intently at the woman he asked to think of one of the cards. He slowly removes two cards from his pocket, but keeps them back toward audience so the faces cannot be seen. He puts these with the deck. That leaves only one card in his pocket—he asks the woman to name the card she is thinking of, then brings the final card out of his pocket. It is, indeed, the thought-of card.

To Prepare

This uses the same principle you have already learned for "Aces Anytime." You can use any deck of cards. Before you begin, secretly remove any two cards from the deck and insert them into the left breast pocket of your shirt, faces toward you (photo 1). You need to be wearing a jacket with an inside breast pocket.

To Perform

Bring out the deck of cards and shuffle it. Turn it facedown and spread it across the table as you ask three people to each choose one card. If you are performing for only one person, have him take out all three cards. If there are two people, have each take one card and you take out the third. Either way, three cards are freely chosen from the

deck. Then, gather the deck and put it into the outer side pocket of your jacket.

Pick up the three chosen cards and hold them in a fan: they're spread, one behind the other (photo 2). Show them all around, then turn to one of the people and ask her to remember one of the cards, but *not* to say the name aloud—*"just think of it."* During all of this you must memorize the order of the three cards. For example, let's assume the six of hearts is on the face of the fan, the five of clubs is in the middle, and the two of clubs is at the back. You must remember all three cards and where they're located. This is pretty simple because they're all different, so just think "six five two, six five two, six five two," and you'll have no trouble. If, on the other hand, two of the cards have the same value, then you must also remember the suit. For example, "six spades, five, six hearts."

Next, turn to another person and say, *"Would you please put your hand into my pocket and feel that it's empty?"* Pull open the left side of your jacket and allow the person to stick his or her hand inside your jacket's inner breast pocket.

Insert the three cards into that pocket, faces toward you, and allow your jacket to close.

Stare intently into the eyes of the woman who is thinking of the card and say, *"Let me try and read your thoughts."* Your right hand ducks into your jacket. Act as if you are inserting your fingers into the jacket pocket containing the deck—but actually insert your thumb into breast pocket of your shirt (photo 3, which is an exposed view—your jacket would not be pulled open in performance). Pull one of the two cards straight up until it completely clears the pocket (but is still hidden by your jacket), then bring it out into view. The card comes out back toward audience as you say, *"No . . . I don't think you picked this card."* Take it with your left hand and place it in your pocket with the deck without letting anyone see its face.

Do the exact same thing again, removing the remaining card from your shirt pocket as if taking it from your jacket pocket. Again study the person's face for a moment, then say, *"No, I don't think it's this one, either."* Transfer the card to your left hand and put in into the pocket with the deck.

Insert your right hand into the inner left breast pocket of your jacket and wait as you say, *"There's only one card left. Let's see if I can read your mind—please name the card you are thinking of."* Now you understand why you need to know the order of the three cards in your pocket—no matter which card she names, that is the card you will pull out of your pocket. In our example, where you're remembering "six five two," you know that the six is the card closest to you, the five is the middle card, and the two is farthest from you. So, whatever card she names, you can easily grasp just that card and bring it out of your pocket.

Hold it back toward the audience as you bring it into view, pause for a second (this creates doubt in the minds of the people watching), then slowly turn the card around to reveal the thought-of card.

38 . —

COLOR BLIND

Criss brings out a box of crayons and hands it to a person who's watching. He turns his back and asks the person to remove any crayon and put it in his hands, which he has put behind his back. Once he has the crayon, Criss turns around to face the person, concentrates for a moment, and is able to tell which color crayon was chosen.

To Prepare

You need a box of crayons: any size is good, but you don't want a gigantic box that has too many different hues of the same color. Criss uses a box of sixteen crayons. The situation in which you're going to perform this trick must not allow people who are watching to see behind you.

To Perform

Say, *"ESP and mind reading are very popular these days."* Turn to a woman who's watching and continue, *"Would you like to try a little experiment in ESP?"* Bring out the box of crayons and say, *"Let's use something simple for our experiment—a box of sixteen crayons, all different colors."*

Give the box to the woman. Watch which hand she takes it with—you need to know if she's right-handed or left-handed. About 90 percent of the population is right-handed, and men are almost two times more likely to be left-handed than woman. That means only a small

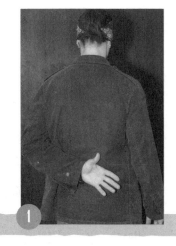

percentage of women are left-handed, so let's assume she takes the box with her right hand.

Say, *"In a moment I'm going to turn my back. Please select any color crayon, remember the color, then hand it to me."* Turn around so you are facing away from the woman. Put your *left* hand behind your back (photo 1).

After she has chosen a crayon and put it in your hand, face forward. Immediately scrape some of the crayon off with your left thumbnail (photo 2). Glance down at her hands and apparently notice, *"Oh—I see that you're right-handed. We really should be in sync here, so let me switch hands."*

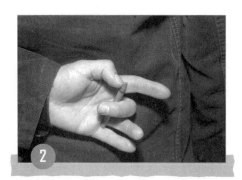

Bring your right hand behind your back and take the crayon from your left hand. Then bring your left hand out and raise it to your head, placing your fingertips on your forehead (photo 3) as you say, *"I'm going to concentrate on the color you chose."* As you raise your hand, glance at your thumbnail and you will clearly see the color of the crayon she chose because of the bit you scraped off (photo 4). Do not pause and stare openly at your thumb! A quick glance as your hand reaches your face will suffice.

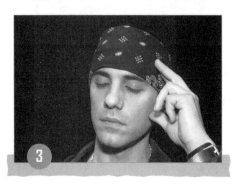

Now that you know the color of the crayon, the rest of the effect is based on presentation. If you simply blurt out the color, it's not nearly as effective as if you make the woman believe that you're unsure at first and are in fact truly reading her mind. I know it sounds silly, but you almost have to believe it yourself in order to make it convincing to everyone else. Let's assume she chose the red crayon.

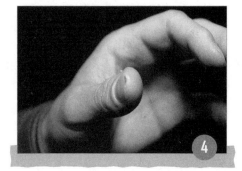

So, start talking, *"I'm getting the impression of a color . . . a dark color . . . a rich color. Warm . . . almost hot . . . not cool . . . not cold . . . I think you chose the red crayon."* After you announce the color, bring your right hand out from behind your back and return the crayon to the woman. Have her put it back into the box and return the box to you.

Now, suppose that it's your lucky day and you happen to choose a left-handed woman . . . what do you do? Simple: if she takes the box of crayons and you realize that she's left-handed, when you turn your back put your *right* hand behind your back to receive the crayon. When you face forward and supposedly notice *at that moment* that she's left-handed, switch hands, bringing your left hand behind your back and your right hand, which has the bit of crayon scraped under the nail, out from behind your back. The rest of the trick works the same way.

39. —

HOUDINI'S FAVORITE TRICK

Criss places a coin under a handkerchief and passes it around so everyone at the table can feel the coin under the handkerchief. A moment after the last person has verified that the coin is under the hanky, Criss tosses the handkerchief into the air and the coin has vanished. His hands are empty.

To Prepare

The preparation for this effect is different from any other you've learned so far: this trick uses an accomplice—someone you've taken into your confidence and who's agreed to help you with the trick in advance. This is an effect to be performed when you are sitting with a group of three to eight people. Your accomplice must be sitting directly to your left. He or she has been asked to do a simple thing: when you extend the handkerchief with the coin beneath it for the accomplice to feel, that person secretly steals the coin.

To Perform

Assume you're going to perform this trick while seated for dinner in either a restaurant or at someone's dining room table. (Either of these are perfect because there'll already be a napkin on the table.)

You're surrounded by a small group of people. Ask one of them if you can borrow a coin and a napkin.

Take the coin and put it under the napkin so it's about in the center. Then, put your hand *above* the napkin and grasp the coin through the cloth. Extend your hand holding the napkin to the person on your right—you are going to work counterclockwise around the table. Ask the first person to put his hand under the hanky and feel that the coin is still there.

Do the same thing with each person in turn, working toward the left and ending with your accomplice. This person appears to do exactly the same thing, but actually takes the coin. The only person who knows this is you, because you can feel it. However, since everyone expects that your accomplice will only feel the coin, no one will suspect that person of actually stealing it.

After your accomplice has made off with the coin, face forward and bring the hanky to the middle of the table. Toss it in the air and let it fall to the table—the coin will have vanished. Allow one of the other people watching to pick up the handkerchief and look underneath it to try and find the coin.

40. ⚊

NO HANDS

Criss begins by explaining that he once saw a card trick done by a man who had no hands. To prove that it isn't impossible, he puts his hands behind his back and says he'll keep them there throughout the entire illusion.

He asks someone to cut the deck and look at the card he or she has cut to. He asks the person to complete the cut, burying the chosen card.

Criss asks the person to cut the deck repeatedly, then turn the deck faceup and cut it some more.

Finally, he asks the person to turn the deck facedown and press lightly on the top. Criss closes his eyes and concentrates for a moment, then announces that the chosen card is a certain number from the top of the deck. The person counts down and finds his card at that number.

To Prepare

Astoundingly enough, you really don't ever touch the deck from the moment this trick begins until it ends. It is necessary, however, to set up the cards in advance. Remove the ace, two, three, four, five, six, seven, eight, nine, and ten of spades from the deck. Arrange the ten cards in numerical order so the ace is at the face of the packet and the ten is at the back (photo 1). With the deck resting face*up* on the table in front of you, simply place those ten cards faceup on the deck. Turn the deck facedown, with the setup cards now on the bottom, and you're ready.

To Perform

Say, *"I once saw a man with no hands do a great trick. You might be wondering how it's possible to do a card trick and never touch the deck—let me show you."* Put your hands behind your back and keep them there throughout the entire trick unless you feel that the spectator doesn't understand something you say and is going to screw things up.

Continue, *"Can you please help . . . ,"* as you gesture toward someone with your head. *"Please cut off about half of the deck—it doesn't have to be exact, of course, just don't cut off a little packet."* Wait until the person does as you ask and cuts off a part of the deck, then say, *"Please put the packet you just cut off on the table next to the rest of the deck.*

"Now, look at the top card of the original packet—the card you cut to." If the spectator doesn't quite understand, you can always bring one of your hands out and point to indicate what you want the person to do. Make sure you never touch the cards.

"Please put the card back on top of the packet you cut off." Once that's been done, say, *"Now complete the cut—in other words, pick up the bottom of the deck and put it on top of your card, burying it."*

Once the person has buried the card in the center, say, *"Good. Now cut the deck—a simple straight cut."* That means that the person should cut a packet off the top of the deck and place it on the table, then put the original bottom half on top of it. You can allow the person to give the deck as many straight cuts as you like. Three or four should be sufficient.

Next, say, *"Please turn the deck faceup."* You are looking for one of the ten spade cards, ace through ten, on the face of the deck. If you see one, then skip to the beginning of the next paragraph and continue. If you do *not* see one, then say, *"Please cut the deck—same way as before."* You must ask the spectator to cut the deck until one of the cuts brings one of your spade cards to the face. It shouldn't take more than two or three cuts. When you see one of your spade cards appear on the face, stop. (If the person who's doing the cutting gets into a rut and keeps cutting the deck and missing the run of spade cards, then you're simply going to have to cut the deck yourself once or twice.)

Ask the person to turn the deck facedown. Say, *"You've got to admit that this could not have been more fair. I've never touched the deck. You cut freely to a card, looked at it, then buried it in the deck. You cut the deck while it was facedown. You cut the deck while it was faceup. Neither of us could possibly have any idea whatsoever where your card is. But the man with no hands knew where my card was."*

Pause for a moment for effect, then continue, *"Turn your hand palm down and press on the top of the deck."* Now let's jump back for a moment—here you must remember exactly which of the ten spade cards you saw on the face of the deck after the cutting. The value of that card indicates exactly how far down in the deck the chosen card is. So, for example, if you saw the five of spades on the face of the deck, the chosen card is now fifth from the top. This is true no matter which of the ten spade cards you saw! If you saw the four of spades, the chosen card is fourth from the top. If you saw the ace of spades, then the chosen card is on top of the deck.

So, assuming you saw the five of spades, you would say, *"Your card is . . . umm . . . five cards down from the top of the deck."* (You name whatever number spade card *you* saw.)

Ask the person to lift cards off the top of the deck one at a time and place them facedown on the table, counting to five, and turn the fifth card faceup. Now is when you may have to bring one of your hands forward, because it's important that the spectator not turn any of the cards he counts off faceup except for the final card. When he turns that card over, people will scream.

Acknowledgments

I extend a special debt of gratitude to my manager and blood brother, Dave Baram, who helped transform my dreams into reality.

To my brothers, Costa and J. D., thank you for being there for me in the best of times and the worst of times. You guys mean more to me than you can ever imagine.

Special thanks to Laura Morton, Mauro DiPreta, Jen Schulkind, Lisa Gallagher, Lynn Grady, Jennifer Slattery, JoAnn, and the entire Winkhart family, Lynn Sarantakos, little Dimitra, George Strumpolis and family, Aunt Stella and Uncle Costa, Abbe Raven, Bob Debitetto, Rob Sharenow, Elaine Frontain-Bryant, Michael Feeney, Melinda McLaughlin, Valerie Albanese, Lori Peterzell, Kerry Tarmey, Nancy Dubuc and everyone at A&E television, Carrot Top, Michael Russo, Felix Rappaport, Tom McCartney, Bill Feldberg, Trish Mittelstadt, Wendie Mosca, John Redman, Letitia Espinoza, Steve Flynn and Ceatta Bogataj, Brad Goldberg, Jenn Michaels and everyone associated with the Luxor and MGM/Mirage Properties, Devra Prywes, John Farrell, Banachek, Johnny Thompson, Mark Cannon, Steve Valentine, Joaquin Ayala, Franz Harary, Jeff McBride, Richiardi, Milt Larson and everyone at the Magic Castle, Michael Mecca, Robert Earl, Jennifer Peterson ("Young

Buck"), Stephanie Lynn Evans, Michael Blum, Michael Yanovich, Toni Lee Roldan ("Cheeks"), Susan Myerberg, Terri Baker, Michael Mazur, Craig Wild, Bob Pozner, Jeffrey Kwatinetz, Jason Verona, Alan Nevins, Marc Pollack, Peter Katsis, Jimmy Bryant and everyone at The Firm, Brooks Litho, Klayton, Peter Thea, Richard Kaufman, Steve Bland, Steve Brooks, Tony Hassini—IMS, Meir Yedid—MagicTimes.com, Yigal Mesika, Monster Music, Richard Osterlind, Steven Brown—Tannen's Magic, Tim Trono—Murphy's Magic Suppliers, Tony Spina, Phil Piacentini—The Magic Shop, Don Wayne, Bob Kohler, Bill Schmeelk—Wellington Enterprises, Scott Interrante, Naveen Jain, Roxanne Pritchard and everyone at Spark Art, the Amazing Jonathan, Lance Burton, Penn & Teller, Bob North, Jim Steinmeyer, Andrew Gerard, Bro Gilbert, Donna Schaefer, John Meyer, Leif Johnson, Clay Patrick McBride, Chris Cassidy, Tom Rutan, Vince and Liah Neil, Count's Kustoms, the Goddards, Adam Mitchell, Micky James, Nicole Vorias, Minx, Hammie, my incredible production team, office staff, and most of all the Loyal fans worldwide—I love you all!

CREDITS

The names of the originators of most of the tricks in this book have been lost over the decades, but we know who created the following miracles, and their names are important.

"Card Thought": The Criss-Cross Force was created by Max Holden.

"Lost and Found": The Cut-Deeper Force was created by Henry Christ; the Deck Toss was created by Jean-Eugene Robert-Houdin.

"Two-Card Monte": Created by Theodore DeLand. The first magician to switch out the gimmicked cards was Don Alan.

"Déjà Vu": Created by Milbourne Christopher.

"Newspaper Prediction": Created by Al Koran.

"Penny or Dime?": Created by Ross Bertram.

"No Hands": Created by Jack Miller.

ABOUT THE AUTHOR

CRISS ANGEL appears on the top-rated series *MINDFREAK*. He has performed more magic on prime-time television in the United States than anyone in history. He has performed on Broadway and in a number of television specials, and has received numerous awards. He is the only person ever to be named magician of the year three times. He lives in Las Vegas and New York City.

LAURA MORTON has collaborated on a number of *New York Times* bestsellers and lives in New York City.